ISBN: 9798673282915

DEDICATION

Dedicated to the wonderful community of poets I discovered on Instagram; a worldwide community of diversity, that is constantly growing, evolving, and thriving. You are the lighthouses that bring my ship to shore. You are part of my daily life, and I treasure you daily.

And to all aspiring poets and writers everywhere; I hope this book, and ongoing project, fills you up and inspires you to new heights.

Yours always,

Ryan Daniel Warner

FOREWORD

The poetry that follows in this; the July's edition of Poetry 365, is a result of the hard work of no less than 110 poets from around the globe; many who have never had work published before. This book serves as an outlet and opening for their talent.

The poetry contained within was originally submitted for my daily poetry prompts featured on my Instagram account, and I felt this work deserved more exposure than the platform of Instagram allows.

In the grand scheme of things; in a world where we are witnessing the horrifying effects of a virus, where we are seeing severe reminders of oppression against our black brothers and sisters, and where war and cruelty continue to dominate, I have very little time for textbook perfection. It means so little in comparison.

As such, this book may be a little rough around the edges. Hell, so am I. And so are you, whenever you truthfully look in a mirror. It's what makes us who we are. A few of these poems may have the odd spelling mistake or grammatical error, and some of them may be less well designed than others, but they are all authentic messages, which we need in this day in age. They contain the powerful, inspiring reminders that we need to take action – be that to try and change others, to change the status quo, or to change ourselves. They remind us to love, they remind us to seek peace; they remind us to fight for what we believe in.

This is poetry. One day at a time. 365 days of the year.

By those who previously didn't have a voice.

By those who matter most.

CONTENTS

FAITH

FAITH
by @poet_in_the_wilderness

Oh me of little faith
For this mustard seed
Is not made to
Move mountains

The only might
It can muster
Will barly force
One feeble foot
In front of

The Other

@Poet_in_the_Wilderness

FAITH
by @writenpoetri

a hand that looks like your own,

would fit right down to the gaps impeccably,

eyes that seem too familiar

to look away from,

an embrace that engulfs,

and all the worries are gone,

there is love in all those things,

not pronounced, not proclaimed

but prevailing anyway,

as she lays under the covers,

a light glow of her phone,

typing away,

and for a while,

there is quiet, in her racing mind,

as part of the world she resides in, sleeps

and she lays awake,

seeking, accepting solace

in temporary gains of a fictional world of her own.

love is solace,

solace is love,

and she compensates

with what she has,

begetting small joys

to last for 24 hours

and two days more,

keeping faith, being patient

to all that remains unfavorable.

  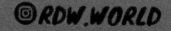

FAITH
by @meremusings33

Its all a leap of faith,
How do you know the Sun
wont fall?
How do you know the clouds
wont blast?
How do you know the Earth
wont recoil?
You dont,
You take a leap of faith.

-Suzu

FAITH
by @fifleuriepoetry

If I could soar up to the clouds,
upon them I would float.
Hope would power my sails,
faith would steer my boat.

On and on I'd travel,
navigating a thunderous course,
Guided by the glow,
of this invisible force.

Shimmering, silver greyness,
angel kisses upon my face,
And if I should return,
I'll tell them-
Heaven is a place.

FIFLEURIEPOETRY

  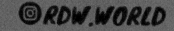

#RDW   WWW.RDW.WORLD   @RDW.WORLD

FAITH
by @realrobdompoetry

I painted you in red sky hues,
Your essence came alive;
We dropped away from worlds we knew,
Our spirits felt revived.
If here among the distant shores
We found out who we are,
Then I would lie forever still
And gaze up at the stars.
See, I have faith in your resolve
And much more than that, dear,
When we're alone you give me light
Where once was only fear.

-Rob Dominick

  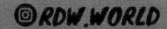

#RDW   WWW.RDW.WORLD   @RDW.WORLD

FAITH
by @mj_notmaryjane

Faith is powerful.

Believing in something,

Or someone.

Looking up to something,

Or someone.

Relying on something,

Or someone.

It's powerful.

Having faith in something,

Or someone,

Means you have a safe place.

It means that thing,

Or that person,

Is your Haven.

Is where you lay all your fears, insecurities, doubts.

You lay it all there because you believe.

Because you have faith.

Faith gives you a friend.

 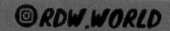

FAITH
by @mrchristophersedgwick

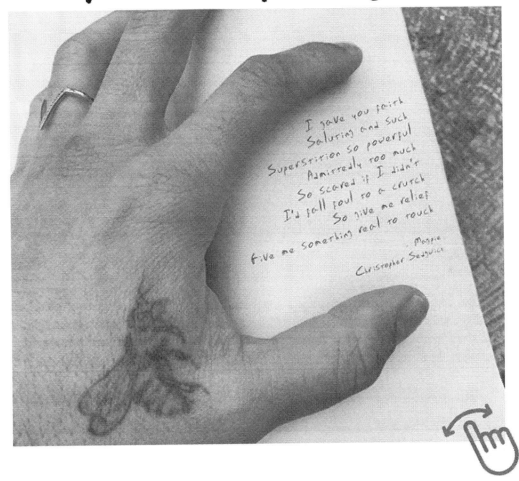

POWER
by @kingizai

The power I thought resided inside
Was never truly mine
You held on to it and sipped on it like a glass of red wine
Intoxicated by what I thought was once mine
Ended up being nothing more then a waste of my time
My love for you could never really subside
But I came to the conclusion it was time to draw the line
What was once divine now a regular woman in my eyes
Now on a solo journey I go
Through the deepest parts of my soul
In search of the power to truly let go
But I'll never truly feel
whole
For my heart comes and goes
With the one woman who took her throne on top my
broken soul.

———

@KingIzai

  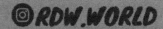

POWER
by @heatherwriting

Fixed for Victory

The unadulterated power required
to hold back the avalanche in my throat
doesn't come to the fainthearted.
I have excavated my own entrails
for my sovereignty.
I have tasted the exsanguinated corpse of war
in ways you could never bear.
Because I believe there are things for which
we are meant to fight.
And more than anything
there is power in belief.
This belief will be sunk into my marrow
long after I am dead.
No amount of purgation
could burn away the immutability of this gospel.

-HK

POWER
by @whatvasthinks

It's like a tug of war
between the hopeless self and the other
reaching for the stars.
I may not fetch all the stars,
but surmounting the forlorn me
gives me the utmost power.

POWER
by @bastianstales

TERRORIZER!
YOU STOLE THE KEYS TO MY POWER
GNAWED AT THE FLESH OF MY SOUL
AND ONCE DEVOURED
SALIVATED FOR MORE
BUT WITH NOTHING LEFT OF MINE
YOU ATE YOUR OWN
THOUGHT BY THOUGHT
I FOUGHT
BUT TOO SOON YOU KILLED ME...
OH!
YOU CANNIBALISTIC MIND OF MINE
WON'T YOU LEARN IN TIME?
I AM YOURS AND YOU ARE MINE!
SO LOVE ME AS YOU SHOULD...
THE WAY I NEVER COULD

BASTIAN

POWER
by @poetstale

Our minds hold so much power
We can quell the raging oceans that we created in the first place
We justify our heinous actions
Then build an inner world of shame
Create chaos on an ordinary Thursday morning
Deceive ourselves to build our pain

On the other hand,
We have the power to extinguish inner fires
We can remove ourselves from our cell and visit the most sacred spaces
Create a powerful love that doesn't exist
Forgive the harshest act
Forgive ourselves
We can set an intention to better all of humanity and carry that with us,
spreading it to every stranger we greet

Imagine the power of our collective minds
Let's set a date, a time, and heal this world
p.s.

POWER
by @emmarosehope

I had the power to survive

To build myself up and strive

To be the best version of me

When everything around me fell apart

I found the strength to get up and start

Fight all the odds and make another day

For any obstacle in my way,

I know I have the power inside me

To be anything I want to be

BLACK

BLACK
by @dianenoirpoetry

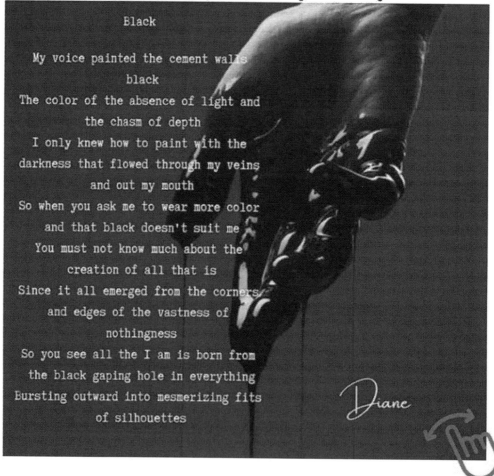

Black

My voice painted the cement walls
black
The color of the absence of light and
the chasm of depth
I only knew how to paint with the
darkness that flowed through my veins
and out my mouth
So when you ask me to wear more color
and that black doesn't suit me
You must not know much about the
creation of all that is
Since it all emerged from the corners
and edges of the vastness of
nothingness
So you see all the I am is born from
the black gaping hole in everything
Bursting outward into mesmerizing fits
of silhouettes

Diane

  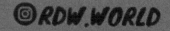

BLACK
by @words_emissions

I was likened to a burnt bread
That the baker forgot in the oven
So I turned out black, looking dead
I hated my skin and my person even

I likened myself to the darkness
Shoot a bullet at me in the night
It'll come back asking for brightness
Cos it can't find me without some light

Will you liken me to who I truly am?
A black, beautiful and bold writer
Defined not by her skin but her charm
A heart of gold, shelled in a black that'll never wither

©words_emissions

 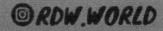

BLACK
by @wildernest_poetry

do not drift calmly past the
current storm of awakening
awareness and reckoning
do not fall back into complacency
in your safe, secure comfortable life
of snow white privilege
do not become silent
do not lose interest, becoming immune
do not become deaf and blind,
failing to hear, see, feel
the sorrowful pain of tortuous death
do not look the other way
do not stop talking, screaming for change
this is not the story of the week,
nor the summer of silence
it must be a lifetime of change
it must bring forth a future of equality and justice
write in on your heart, soul, words, actions
black lives matter
then, now, always

Michelle @wildernest_poetry

#RDW   WWW.RDW.WORLD   @RDW.WORLD

BLACK
by @poetry_by_varsha

BLACK, WHITE AND MORE

How would the world be
If black and white was all that we could see
Would we still look up to see the sky
Without its canvas of blues and reds passing by
Would we still fill our vases with flowers
Without their colours to brighten up our idle hours
Would we still hold onto jewels red and green
Without their precious glint to lure us in
Would we still have dresses by the dozen
Without the playful problem to choose between dark red and darker red
Would looking out of a window bring us the same joy
Without the pops of random greens and browns to enjoy
Would our moods still swing to and fro
Without the reds to colour our anger and our envy green
Would there be inspiration to be found
Without colours flooding our senses and lurking around
How would the world be
If there were no colours to set us free
Would the world be a black and white whirlwind of gloom?
Maybe yes, if beauty was limited to what our eyes see
Would the world not care and be happy just the same?
Maybe yes, if beauty lies in what our souls feel

- Varsha Bondada

BLACK
by @nabeel.mohan

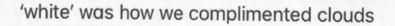

in the old country
the mud and tree trunks were brown

nights for star-gazing were
deepest black

'white' was how we complimented clouds

the sun shone yellow as it
burned our backs

red was blood and heart, both proud

but now, in this land,
colour is you and me, bound.

 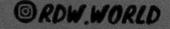

BLACK
by @dr.inkwright

"Brown x Black"

My skin is dark brown, but they call me black
A fact based upon racial divide, to deprive
several cultures of people of wealth &
resources
They forced it upon their own
Killed many of us before camera existed
Honed in on their greed & corruption to
disrupt any form of peace my people had
It's so bad that many who aren't like me can
see the unworthy ones holding guns in the
faces of women & children
The impact of jealousy, greed, and wanting to
be superior beings
Isn't just racist whites vs blacks
It's the disruption of peace to appease the
need to feed their greed

– @dr.inkwright (7/3/2020)

BLACK
by @s.i.m.true

I used to try to drink all my sorrows away.

All my anger and all my sadness in the hope

to feel some love again.

I drank and drank. Until my lights went out

and only total *blackness* was left.

Nothing to feel, nothing to hear and

nothing to see.

I felt at peace in this pitch-black world.

s.i.m.true

BLACK
by @lismcdermott

Nineteen-sixty-eight, two American athletes
Shocked the wolrd,
Raised their fists with a Black Power salute,
A cry for freedom and for human rights.
Now in 2020, we are still battling this fight.
Watching then and watching still
I've had my fill of discrimination
That is affecting all the world; every nation.
Black is beautiful was another nineteen-sixties cry
Although sadly, not acknowledged by everyone's eye.
There is no God-given right for one race
To be the more privileged face;
We should all be working for equality,
Putting down those who show their ignorance with ferocity.
Remember, we all have one thing in common
We are all human, sharing a huge part of our DNA.
Brown, white, olive, black
For our future, let's get us on the right track.

©Lis McDermott 202?

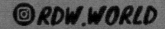

BLACK
by @littleblackheartpoetry

Dear Black,

How are you today? Are you holding up ok? Are you ready to face the fight. Stand up and scream for your rights! Tell the world that #blacklivesmatter? Because today is a new day and it must be told again. You must wake up everyday and not give up. I know you are tired. I know you are scared. Scared for your brothers, sisters and children. But I will be there for you. Fighting alongside you. Screaming with you. #blacklivesmatter! Let our voices be heard. We will win. We have to. There is no option.

In solidarity,

M

PEACOCK

PEACOCK
by @xharhwrites

Like a peacock you pride yourself
in your beauty but it's your
heart that I crave
Staring at your face perfection is
what I see and I swear there's
nothing I'd change
The love I have for you
transcends your body
and pours into the depths of your
soul,
For one day I hope that I'd get
the priviledge to call you my own

  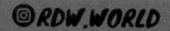

PEACOCK
by @nabeel.mohan

my grandfather had wild peacocks
on his land
For years, as children, we'd wander,
hoping to steal glances
at posing, primpy males
in the throes of dance.

years later, others came too -
posing, primpy males,
in smart suits
and colourful ties,
with pens and paper
and company lies.

No more land,
no more peacocks.
nothing left to see -
except a city-bound man
who's feathers stayed fanned
in a dance that lasted
till a hundred and three

PEACOCK
by @kipyard.rudling

PEACOCK = [PEA(HEN WON THE ANNUAL RAIN DANCE COMPETITION FOR THE SECOND TIME IN A ROW, ADDING ANOTHER FEROCIOUS FEATHER TO HER ALREADY ILLUSTRIOUS CAP, BUT WAS UPSET WITH HER SIGNIFICANT OTHER FOR TURNING UP TO THE EVENT DRUNK ON GREY GOOSE, AND BEHAVING LIKE AN ABSOLUTE) COCK]

- KR

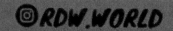

#RDW   WWW.RDW.WORLD   ©RDW.WORLD

PEACOCK
by @newkirk.jon

The peacock took flight to roost
just before dusk in the cypress
tree under the corn husk moon.
The turquoise light, the turquoise
feathers, almost dream-like, that
existed together just before the
night was set to bloom.

– – JnNwkrk

PEACOCK
by @beboldtoya

graceful elegant strides
met wandering eyes
emotions beat in her flirtatious
playful smile
illustrious beauty
with an expressive laughter
A
modern siren
statuesque woman
she fed her preys shimmers
of hope with her bright personality
IN
her blue green flamboyant
dress like a PEACOCK train
she was the center of attention
in the ballroom
men treated her like a deity
women looked at her with envy

MIRROR
by @mind_itches

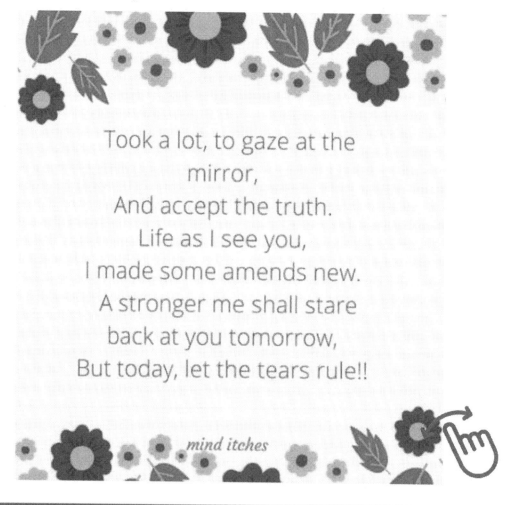

Took a lot, to gaze at the
mirror,
And accept the truth.
Life as I see you,
I made some amends new.
A stronger me shall stare
back at you tomorrow,
But today, let the tears rule!!

mind itches

MIRROR
by @d_b1226

WE ARE MIRRORS

WHAT YOU THINK OF ME IS YOU
WHAT I THINK OF YOU IS ME

NOW THAT YOU SEE WHAT YOU
DON'T LIKE IN YOURSELF
REFLECTED IN ME-

YOU BECOME A POWERFUL
TOOL OF CHANGE FOR
YOURSELF

DB

  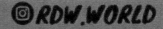

MIRROR
by @tb.finch

if we are a looking-glass
mirroring those who shaped us

then the only reason that my pane
is strong enough for this task

is because of the ferocity and strength
of the women i am reflecting

- tb finch

  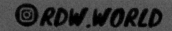

MIRROR
by @wordsbykerry

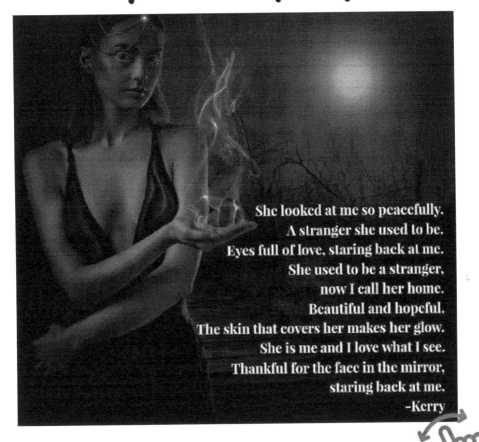

She looked at me so peacefully.
A stranger she used to be.
Eyes full of love, staring back at me.
She used to be a stranger,
now I call her home.
Beautiful and hopeful.
The skin that covers her makes her glow.
She is me and I love what I see.
Thankful for the face in the mirror,
staring back at me.

–Kerry

MIRROR
by @whatvasthinks

Yesterday morning when I saw my mirror,
I saw a lovely woman with a smile.
She looked beautiful, so she felt wonderful
and she behaved gracefully.
Throughout the day, great and unpleasant
moments had their share.
But she hooked on to the things that didn't go well,
letting go the hope and goodness,
the rest of the day could have offered.
Had she been optimistic, the woman in the mirror
would have still been beautiful
and would have greeted me goodnight,
with a SMILE.

WhatVasThinks

MIRROR
by @autumnalfyre

I once trapped a spirit
In the full-length mirror
Hanging on the back of my door
Looking unchanged through ages
She was the spirit of youth
Always showing me a face I'd used before
Frozen in time, my image lacked truth
I let the spirit go and accepted beauty's changes
If I face age, maybe I won't fear it
And I'll see myself a little clearer

 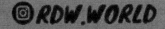

MIRROR
by @s.i.m.true

When I'm getting dressed or undressed somewhere where men and women can see me,

I want them to be curious.

When they see the back of my body I want them to see my beautiful legs that's carrying my voluptuous buttocks first. I'm wearing lingerie that is accentuating the roundness of this divine body part. Accentuating my wide hips and slim waistline. When they look at me I want their eyes to move upward. Drawn by the lingerie I'm wearing. It's inviting them to follow my beautiful back upward my neck.

I know that you're looking.

So I made sure that my hair is on one side, revealing the neck you may kiss in your fantasies. I know you're curious. I know that you're waiting for me to turn around. But I'll let you wait and enjoy the view for a bit longer. Because I don't have that privilege when I'm looking in the mirror.

 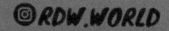

MIRROR
by @mj_notmaryjane

We all want to see what we look like,

Each time we look in the mirror.

And every single time,

We're disappointed by what we see.

But the mirror's just doing it's job.

The mirror's just putting it out there like it is.

The mirror doesn't bullshit.

The mirror doesn't hide anything.

The mirror gives as it sees.

You know, maybe we should all be like the mirror.

MIRROR
by @petren33

Mirror
I walk past my mirror everyday,
I used to glance at myself in it,
But now I can't bare to see my reflection.
My mirror sees everything,
It sees my smile starting to shatter,
My belly becoming flatter,
The thoughts of 'do I matter'.
The mirror wishes it could tell me how beautiful I am,
But it can't,
So it just sits there, leaning against my bedroom wall, in silence.

EAGLE
by @lionelspeaks

Eagle

You say I'm flying...I call it soaring.
High above all...the thought of never
coming down is so alluring.
I can see all from here...though I know it's
much larger than it appears.
This is a big big place...but I'm free to
catch the wind and glide at my own pace.
Between the blue and brown...as these
blissful winds move me around.
With so much freedom and so much
peace...my excited heartbeat is the only
sound.
I wish I could bring you with me...this
gorgeous view is so profound...

EAGLE
by @chrislpoetry

Eagle

Over mountain tops, ever so high

The eagle soars through the sky

One glimpse of movement below

Diving for its prey, not just show

One quick swoop and away it goes

Onto its lair, the eagle never slows

EAGLE
by @patriciahelenwriter

Full-bellied fueled
With waterfowl and field mice
The regal raptor rides the wind
Circling ceremonial cedarwood fire
As worshippers gather in reverence
Calling in supplication to the talon-titan
With ancestral melodies played on flutes
And on whistles carved from eagle bones
Then...worshippers absorb a rippled silence
Anticipating the swoop of creator's messenger

The eagle's expansive wingspan kites
In magnificence of might and splendor
Breathtaking in hypnotic elastic suspension-
Then with controlled slow-motion precision
Its muscular legs straighten and talons unclasp
And in majesty and with calculated grace
The bird alights on 60-foot twisted arbutus
Rooted on the periphery of the gathering
And feathered in courage and in wisdom
The eagle watches and waits and watches

  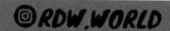

EAGLE
by @kipyard.rudling

EAGLE = [EAG(ER AND MAJESTIC, SHE SOARED HIGH IN THE CLEAR BLUE SKY, WHILE HER PREY BELOW, PRAYED FOR HIS DEAR LIFE, GRIPPING TIGHTLY ONTO HIS BIB)LE]

- KR

EAGLE
by @namans_words

What do I have that you don't?
I set my eyes on what I want,
undeterred, persistently unperturbed,
and you?
I face my storms, however gigantic,
head-on, vigorously afraid,
and you?

I revive myself, when down and out,
confidently with firm resolves,
and you?
I use whatever I have,
to be anything I want to be,
and you?

Look within and you will know ,
you have everything that I do.
Believe in yourself and you'll be
your own hero,
your own *eagle*.

©naman

EAGLE
by @dr.inkwright

"Like the Eagle"

I am fearless
I take that which I please
Free to fight for the freedom I am owed
Not simply because I am grown
But because I am one who is known to seek out what is
morally right
So I'm taking this frame of time
Allowing tongue to give sound to sound the battle cry
Whether in the heat of midday or cool of the night
I am no fool
I know what I fight for
Have you not heard the details of the eagle's eye?
They have vast levels of sight
...I see you
But in my fight to stand on the right side
You cannot see what you're doing wrong
When you shout & play the racist song

Jose V. Wright, Jr.
@dr.inkwright (7/6/2020)

 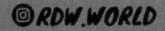

RISE
by @namans_words

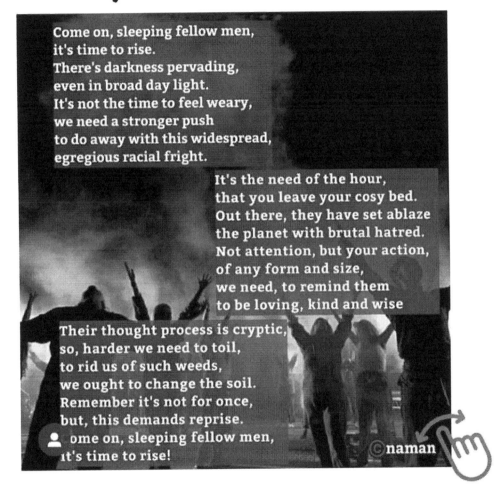

Come on, sleeping fellow men,
it's time to rise.
There's darkness pervading,
even in broad day light.
It's not the time to feel weary,
we need a stronger push
to do away with this widespread,
egregious racial fright.

It's the need of the hour,
that you leave your cosy bed.
Out there, they have set ablaze
the planet with brutal hatred.
Not attention, but your action,
of any form and size,
we need, to remind them
to be loving, kind and wise

Their thought process is cryptic,
so, harder we need to toil,
to rid us of such weeds,
we ought to change the soil.
Remember it's not for once,
but, this demands reprise.
Come on, sleeping fellow men,
it's time to rise!

©naman

RISE
by @akingspoet

It was July
and the heat r o s e
from the earth
like a steamy sigh
still drunk
on the furied touch
of summer rain.

a.king

 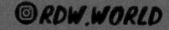

RISE
by @tb.finch

a puddle for far too long
now i bask where i lie

no more pounding rain
no more trampling heels

my pain will evaporate into the sky
feel my steam
as i rise

- tb finch

RISE
by @samantha_peterson_poetry

Baking Bread

I roll you around like dough in my hands
I knead you
And knead you
Until you meet my demands
Then wait
Ever so patiently
As you rise and grow before me
I see you transform
Into more than you were
Bracing yourself for my oven apurr
I insert you slowly, so not to get burned
And you bake and you brown
and you rise up some more
I feel the heat rising, the pressure is high
I salivate smelling your aroma of rye
So close to complete, so close to the feast
I long for a taste of your softness so sweet
And when you are risen as high as you'll go
And the heat has embedded in your flaky dough
When I am satisfied with your golden roll
I'll pull you out slowly and devour you whole

- Samantha Peterson

 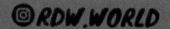

RISE
by @saharjaan_

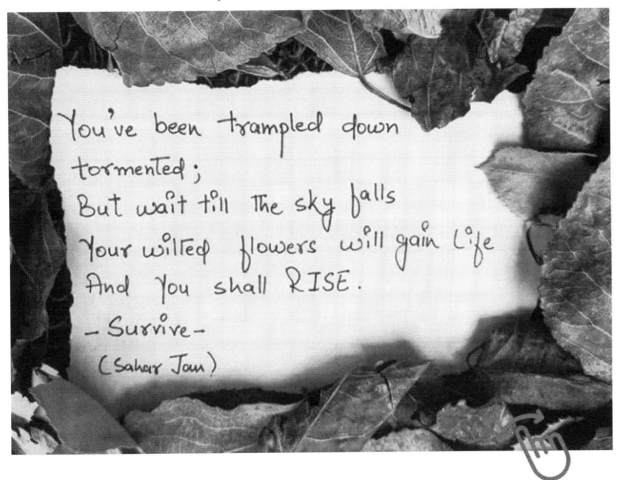

You've been trampled down
tormented;
But wait till the sky falls
Your wilted flowers will gain life
And you shall RISE.
— Survive —
(Sahar Jaan)

RISE
by @hear_me_say

This constant pain
and endless suffering,
makes her feel
alone, standing in the dark rain
with no umbrella to shield on,
at one second,
she can feel cold crippling in her veins,
devouring her black heart,
the next second,
she feels the burning desire
to swallow all her pain,
with stubbornness inside each cell,
she will stand up each time she falls,
even if she'll burn to ashes,
with courage she'll endure it all,
and then accepting who she is,
she'll rise in those ashes above all,
floating in the sky,
one day
she will,
rise above the all the labelled heights,
rise from the bottom,
like a bird soaring the damn skies 🦋

RISE
by @paulrkohn

Hurting people hurt people, hurting people hurt people, hurting people hurt people,

And I don't want to hurt you ever...

As I'm on my path to strength, I heed all I have learned, all that's been asked of me.

I step back to give space, I silence up.

Left beaten, battered, bloodied, betrayed, I'm still here with trust, patience, hope and love, and I will rise.

Cos Hurting people hurt people, hurting people hurt people,

And I refuse to do that...

So I'll build myself back up brick by brick by brick by brick by brick, by brick, by brick,

Until I'm so grounded that I am unshakeable, unmoveable, steadfast, strong once again...

Cos hurting people hurt people...

But I? I will no longer hurt...

I will heal, unwavering in my strength

I will rise, stronger than ever...

No longer invisible, I will shine just as bright!

Paul R Kohn

RISE
by @itsme_maximus

I say to you brother, RISE.
For the battle is not over yet.
Till we all have transcended above.

But here on Earth, I say.
Rise above all negativities.
In the moments of helplessness,
I say.
Rise above despair and unto hope.

Thrill yourself.
Heal your mind.
And stand tall as if on a hill.
Things may rise and fall,
But I say to you brother.
RISE NOW NEVER TO FALL AGAIN.

©B. Maximus U

  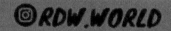

#RDW   WWW.RDW.WORLD   RDW.WORLD

RISE
by @kingdomherrmann

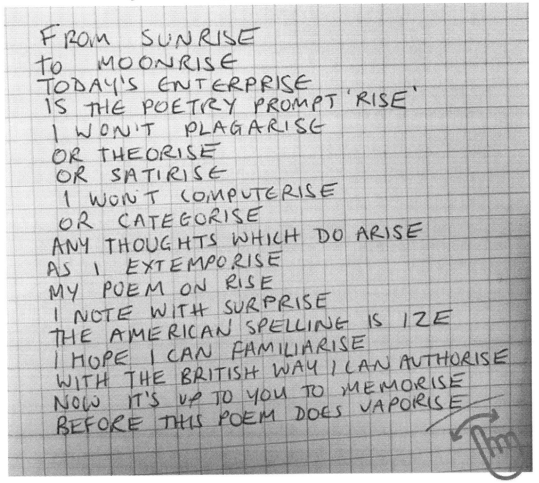

FROM SUNRISE
TO MOONRISE
TODAY'S ENTERPRISE
IS THE POETRY PROMPT 'RISE'
I WON'T PLAGARISE
OR THEORISE
OR SATIRISE
I WON'T COMPUTERISE
OR CATEGORISE
ANY THOUGHTS WHICH DO ARISE
AS I EXTEMPORISE
MY POEM ON RISE
I NOTE WITH SURPRISE
THE AMERICAN SPELLING IS IZE
I HOPE I CAN FAMILIARISE
WITH THE BRITISH WAY I CAN AUTHORISE
NOW IT'S UP TO YOU TO MEMORISE
BEFORE THIS POEM DOES VAPORISE

RISE
by @nasir_beyg

Holding one end of the broken string
We watch silence dwindle in the sky
Like a kite no more attached to the thread
Swaying with the wind of breaths
Descending gradually; bit by bit
We hold our breaths
So it does not get stuck in the trees of insecurities
Hoping it steers clear of pylons of fears
And lands on the soil of love in our souls
I don't know if it is me or you
One of us has become anxious and start breathing
heavily
As it soars and rises higher and higher
And gets stuck in a broken star
Now at night it shines in the sky
Making us sad and smile at once
Because we know though it twinkles
It is ours no more; it will never land in our souls
It has drifted lightyears away
And all we hold on to is a broken end of string
@nasir_beyg

#RDW   WWW.RDW.WORLD   ⊙RDW.WORLD

PROTEST

PROTEST
by @poetstale

People
Rise
Omnipotent
To
Eradicate
Segregationist
Traditionalism

P R O T E S T

  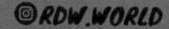

PROTEST
by @poetrybyparkes

I protest
I stand up for love
Feelings and emotions
And all the things we can't speak of

I protest
Against internal conflict
Self-flagellation of souls
And the beings that made us addicts

I protest
Whilst standing tall
With no quarter given
And for those who gave it their all

I protest
In the name of serenity
For a clear mind and a pure heart
We stand together for you and me

PROTEST
by @j.wildepoetry

THE DISPROPORTIONATE BRUTALITY AND
FATALITIES AGAINST OUR COMMUNITIES OF
COLOR HAS GOT TO STOP.
WE THE PEOPLE HAVE BEEN PROTESTING IN THE
STREETS,
BECAUSE THERE HAVE BEEN TOO MANY BODIES
LEFT THERE TO BLEED.
AUTHORITIES NEED TO BE HELD ACCOUNTABLE
FOR THEIR ACTIONS, BECAUSE THERE IS NO
TAKING A LIFE AND THEN ASKING FOR A
RETRACTION.

BLACK LIVES MATTER

~J. Wilde

PROTEST
by @jbpoetry1

The masses are stirring
Unease on the streets
Something's afoot
a rumble of feet

Spreading like wildfire
Injustice, unfair
Are the words that I'm hearing
The people despair

A letter to Boris
Is written post haste
And to all the MPs
who govern this place

Will we succeed
in righting this wrong
If not we'll protest
And all bang our gong.

JB

  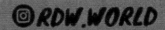

PROTEST
by @patriciahelenwriter

Political despots and thugs align
Socio-moral codes are redefined
People detained and restrained
People demoralized and defamed
Corruption is the enforced norm
Catalyzing need for social reform
Protestors gather because of unrest
Protestors motivated by distress
A mandate to visibly rise to action
Gives voice to their dissatisfaction

Protest is imperative for movement
Protest is imperative for improvement
Protest is witnessed in a public forum
Protest executed in respectful decorum
Protest in marches and in publications
Protest in song and poetry persuasion
Protest is both a freedom and a right
Protest is a redemptive beacon of light

PROTEST
by @words_emissions

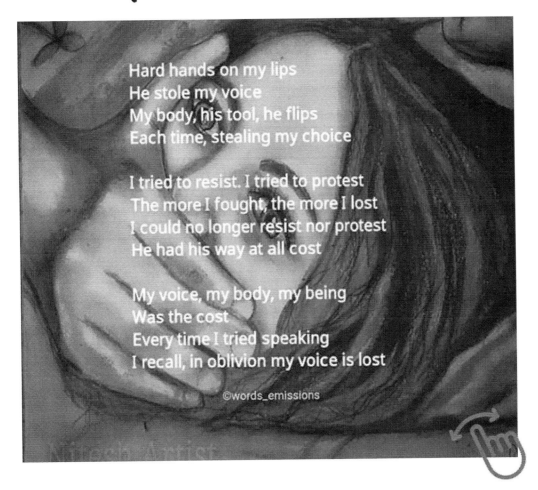

Hard hands on my lips
He stole my voice
My body, his tool, he flips
Each time, stealing my choice

I tried to resist. I tried to protest
The more I fought, the more I lost
I could no longer resist nor protest
He had his way at all cost

My voice, my body, my being
Was the cost
Every time I tried speaking
I recall, in oblivion my voice is lost

©words_emissions

PROTEST
by @caitlinjadepoetry

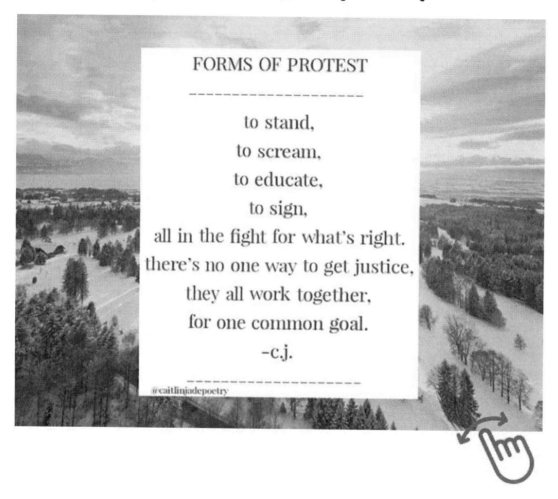

FORMS OF PROTEST

to stand,
to scream,
to educate,
to sign,
all in the fight for what's right.
there's no one way to get justice,
they all work together,
for one common goal.

–c.j.

@caitlinjadepoetry

MOUNTAIN
by @samyukta_81d

The two of us, we shared a dream
Of love, of courage, of might;
And arm-in-arm we set off
To conquer the mountain of life.

Although the journey is brutal,
The chasms formidably steep;
I know one day we'll watch the sunrise
Standing victorious on the peak.

~Asta

MOUNTAIN
by @jbpoetry1

Awe-inspiring mountain,
born of mother earth,
majestic and panoptic,
mighty and diverse,
as a sentinel you stand,
with your weather-beaten slopes,
a passenger of the ages,
outlasting all our hopes,
until the ends of time,
when all will cease to be,
guardian of the earth,
throughout all history.

JB

MOUNTAIN
by @awaywithwordscal

She stands tall, beautiful
A vision.
Throughout the seasons
Her beauty changes;
Summer brings an adornment of green;
Sun at her top, she basks in the warmth.
Families trail up and down,
Picnics and photographs,
Laughter till sunset.
Autumn welcomes the wild Welsh winds;
Leaves of amber and orange hues
Dance upon the barren ground.
Through a bitter winter
Her peak cloaked in white
Concealing her weathered terrain.
Danger and death
Clouds descend as a warning
Of perilous pilgrimages.
By spring, new life
Lambs prance, butterflies dance
And the birds sing out in symphony.
The ground awakens,
Colours bloom.

#RDW   WWW.RDW.WORLD   ⊙RDW.WORLD

MOUNTAIN
by @autumnalfyre

MOUNTAINS

As writers we form mountains,
building them when we put words on the page,
day after day, again and again

We shape the landscape.
From the view at the peak, readers seek truth
or just entertainment and mindless escape

On these mountains, new ideas grow like trees
and fragile creatures make their homes
from words we write born of daydreams

MOUNTAIN
by @kingofthedomain

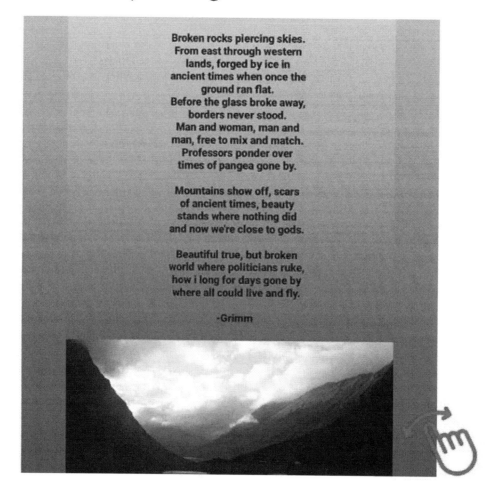

Broken rocks piercing skies.
From east through western
lands, forged by ice in
ancient times when once the
ground ran flat.
Before the glass broke away,
borders never stood.
Man and woman, man and
man, free to mix and match.
Professors ponder over
times of pangea gone by.

Mountains show off, scars
of ancient times, beauty
stands where nothing did
and now we're close to gods.

Beautiful true, but broken
world where politicians ruke,
how i long for days gone by
where all could live and fly.

-Grimm

MOUNTAIN
by @kuranya_a_poet_dreaming

she looks
at the mountain ahead
unclimbable; impassable
full of sheer faces and jagged rocks
and she wonders how
she will ever reach the top
with no harness and no ropes to steady her
still she climbs; alone
sometimes breathless and afraid
one tentative step at a time
until she reaches the top
the mountain now insignificant
in her fight for life

#RDW   WWW.RDW.WORLD   @RDW.WORLD

MOUNTAIN
by @mj_notmaryjane

This thing between us,

This constant bickering,

This loud silence,

This heartbreaking healing,

that we both feel we have to do.

This ominous presence,

This transparent wall,

because we both know there's someone on
the other side,

we only have to reach out.

But we don't.

We don't reach out,

Because there is a mountain between us.

  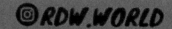

JOY

JOY
by @poetstale

Joy

Mirriam says *joy* is a state of felicity

Joy is a friend to me

The first two sips of great wine

A conversation that lights up your eyes

It's the best night of your life

A shooting star glimpsed in a crystal clear sky

A moment in time / Of natural highs

The feeling you get when you did it *just right*

Your favorite song coming on in the car

with the windows down and you're singing out loud

The first step on the beach that first day of vacation

Seeing your love when you get to the station

It's fleeting, it passes, like the most beautiful sunset

But these brief, precious moments live on in your heart

p.s.

  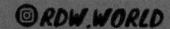

JOY
by @emmarosehope

The pain.

Unbearable, but barely felt while I was

focused on the thought of it all being over

The sweat dripping from my face, my hair.

Ripping me apart at the seams as those

final contractions tore through me like

blades

Then,

It stopped. Placed in my arms, this tiny

human and, as I met the eyes of this little

human boy

My heart was filled with pure, unfiltered

joy

 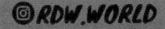

JOY
by @wenbae

Joy.

A committed emotion felt by all
Opening gates and breaking down walls.

Some find it in remembering the past
Others find it at the bottom of a glass.

To grab hold and keep on its track
To get the spark in our eyes back.
To climb and reach its peak
To put dimples back on our cheeks.
To test the waters and to swim
To merit ourselves with a grin.

We strive to meet its every requirement
Whatever it takes to feel content.

We conjure in our blood, sweat and not to be coy-
Theres a reason they call call it 'tears of joy'

JOY
by @itsme_maximus

What happened to joy?
Everyone seems so depressed.
Always recalling pain
And those who hurt them.

What happened to the joy
Of having friends?
What happened to the joy
Of making good memories?
And what happened to the joy
Of being in love?

Let us remember that our joy,
Can only be created by us.
Let us fill the whole essence
Of our living, with joy.
And pray we attain
The utmost joy of heaven.

(C)B. Maximus U

JOY
by @hi_cool_dapoet

Finally   @hi_cool_dapoet
I can truly smile without manipulating my
lips into curving
Today
the mirror reflects a joyful soul
no longer am I a man broken and hurting
Life
who knew choosing everyone over
yourself can led to loosing yourself
The day I dedicated my time to me
I found peace
I fell in love with the person I never took
time to meet
and
I gotta say he's cool as fuck
I once was happy pleasing everyone but
I found joy in learning who I am and what I
need in life to consistently stay at peace

  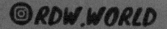

JOY
by @j.wildepoetry

Joy.
Life sprinkles droplets of joy even though
the world may be stormy.

Like the way I catch you staring at me or the
way you remember to bring me coffee.
I also enjoy the way you bring me my
favorite wine and snack without me asking.
My favorite droplets are the way you sing
our daughter to sleep and the way in the day
you keep her laughing.

These are the droplets of joy that help make
the rainbow in this storm called life.

~J. WILDE

 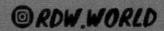

#RDW WWW.RDW.WORLD @RDW.WORLD

JOY
by @_ashley_words

The flying elephants

The exquisite grin on a tot's face
comes in all sizes, colours and shapes.
Light as a feather they feel,
a heart as heavy they lift with
all our insecurities and paranoia
dissipating in moments we see a balloon fly
high above the grounds where we stand,
tormented and young but still feels old,
old enough to not clap in joy when we see
a balloon fly high like we once did when
dad took us to fairs.
A few leap years apart we grew
up to lose all our childhood charms but
today as I sit with my beloved in one such
fair, hand in hand so in love, old enough to
not jump with joy but we still do anyway
when we see a balloon fly past us,
a heart shaped one in red cause even the little
things feels beautiful in love and rightly so
and as we turned around to walk home,
we saw a sky so full of those varying
inflated bags, I call them flying elephants
all free and happy wanting to be taken
home for people to fall in love again
with the little things in life.

JOY
by @hl_ridge

Mud-stained Jeans
Stampeding cowboy boots
Call out the cavalry.
Tousled dirty-blonde curls
That irresistible smile
In their own little world.
Car sounds perfected
Dinos ruled the earth
Sweet changes unexpected.
Oh but those blue eyes
Sheepish beneath long lashes
Would get me every time.
Let's blow bubbles
Travel to the moon
Mischievous, a.k.a. trouble.
Their hearts unlike any other
Tender, caring and kind
So proud to be their mother.
When they call you by that name
Your heart swells to almost bursting
Unsure what you did to deserve the same.
Little hands trust in yours
Laughter so abundant
Love seeping from every pore.
I have scarcely found more joy
In any other soul or creature
Than I have in my little boys.

H.L. Ridge

  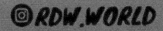

JOY
by @debbie_o_bottled_up_feelings

SILENT GARDENS
BRING ME NO JOY.
I WANT TO SIT IN THE SUN
AND SING.
I WANT TO BE IN LOVE
AND HEAR SONGBIRDS
SING ME LOVE SONGS
IN THE GENTLE BREEZE.

HOLIDAY

HOLIDAY
by @emmarosehope

Along the narrow, winding paths of my
dreams
I see myself travelling to the outer edges of
the earth
Learning about every person, religion and
culture
And see this world for what it's truly worth
I want a holiday of indulgence, but not like
you'd think
A spiritual overload, and not one of food
and drink
Along the narrow, winding paths of my
dreams
I long for a holiday that makes my heart
overflow at the seams

HOLIDAY
by @patriciahelenwriter

HOLIDAY

Time away
Time to play
Tour package sold
9 to 5 grind on hold
Suitcases cram-packed
Departure right on track
Everyone buckled in the car
Airport location not too far
Final destination is overseas
Full itinerary includes 4 countries
Everyone's expectations run high
Though one kid is terrified to fly
Up ... up ...and away
Beginning of our family holiday
A time ripe with incredible discovery
To be followed by pocketbook recovery

HOLIDAY
by @newkirk.jon

```
The holiday season
built for centuries
built off tradition
build a fire
for my attention
pick through some stars
enclose a letter
                    cut to
put up a tree, decorate
This alley of darkness
the underworld blooms
The snow falls late afternoon
            The music proceeds
The classics
Celebrate a fable at the table
worshiping the light, our saviour
our dreams of tomorrow
The glow, the light, the rise
            we celebrate
The sun is back from the dead


            - - JnNwkrk
```

  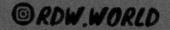

HOLIDAY
by @poetstale

New Holiday

Let's choose a day, a holiday

Let's call it *Humanity Day*

And on this day let us all treat each other the way we'd like to

be treated

Let's all take care of each other

A worldwide day of truce and prayer and kindness

No presents, no Hallmark cards, no guilt, no unworthy feelings,

no shame

A day of the best of humanity

And maybe we'll feel a shift in the world

Maybe we'll enjoy it so much that we'll do it more than once a

year

Maybe we can start with Humanity Day

p.s.

HOLIDAY
by @words_emissions

I need some time off
Life is too exhausting
I'm asking for a time out
But life doesn't take a break
Does she?

I'm tempted to run off
To a place soothing
To clear my thoughts out
A holiday could be the prefect break
Will she?

©words_emissions

  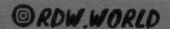

HOLIDAY
by @wenbae

Holiday

Crystal clear seas met with golden grain
Where breakfast is lunch accompanied with
champagne.
A day of no thoughts, no worries, no strife
And nights that bring memories for life.

Even the man on the moon seems happier, the
stars a little brighter
And this all inclusive package will make your
clothes tighter.

Family photos and funny drawings on the pier
Visiting numerous gift shops to find the perfect
souvenir.

At a blink the holiday has come to pass
No time to think, got a plane to catch.
Back home summer isn't the same, sunbathing in
the yard. But I'll have those memories and a
postcard.

-Wendy

HOLIDAY
by @alyssenatali

In the crashing waves, we were floating
How did we get here? Underneath these fiery
summer lit skies
The green seafoam brushed up on the shore,
exploding
Into the grooves of the sunset kissed sand,
spinning clockwise
Your eyes, deeper than a trench, thoughts
you were provoking
Filled with emotions that can play anyone
faster than a violin
Your lips so perfectly shaped, like the heart
your soul craves
Your glisten with every drop that drips, down
your porcelain skin
I can hear your heart beating, through the
ripples now engraved
At this moment, on this holiday, where we
first met in sin
-a. natali

 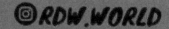

HOLIDAY
by @tharbeland

"Holiday"

Some days spent outside,
Can be considered a holiday.
Self-care, tying together ties,
Bridges built, sometimes with splinters
abound,
A reason to celebrate.
Piecing perfectly placed puzzles promptly,
Today, does it last forever?
Do you want it to extend to a few more
sunrises?
It's more than the thrill of the hunt and
search.
It's much bigger than skyscrapers kissing
clouds.
("And so, the narrator learns that today is
today...")
I miss the sound of time, when you're in
suspended serenity,
I think upon a holiday, we're meant to look
back at it,
So that we have something in our vision,
To see and look back at.
(holidays are holidays, my friend)
Can we make memories for many more
moments?

HOLIDAY
by @awaywithwordscal

Every now and then
I wish for ONE day.
ONE day for ME.
A mummy's holiday.
I love my kids to the moon,
But in truth...
I'm going to blow real soon!
Mummy needs a holiday!
The dirty faces, bloodied knees,
Bike rides, walks and climbing trees.
Thousands of discarded meals,
Lie uneaten,
Heathens.
That mountain of washing
Each day at its peak;
The hoovering, dusting
Every day of the week!
So kids, I implore you...
Just give me ONE day!
Please, let mummy have a holiday!

LUNGS
by @lismcdermott

The manacled, chained and enslaved who fought to be free,
They breathed
Those who fought their way out through the mustard gas at Flanders Field,
They breathed
The men emerging, face blackened by coal dust from the bowels of the earth,
They breathed
The people of colour killed when held by police with inordinate force,
Unable to breathe
Those who died in the preventable tradegy of the Grenfell fire,
Unable to breathe
The thousands around the world who protested against racism,
We breathe
Those who care about environment change and the earth,
We breathe
Those of us who continually fight against inequality and oppression,
We breathe
The reason to keep living and confront the struggles of life,
We breathe
For our children, grandchildren and future generations,
We breathe

© Lis McDermott 2020

LUNGS
by @_tabishj

I'll keep you alive,
Alive in my poetry
Make you breathe
the same oxygen,
Until you can inflate
no more

tabish. J

LUNGS
by @kingofthedomain

Baby screams, muscles swell, oxygen rich
and expand the chest, the first sign of life,
that precious wail. A smile approaches with
sighs of gratitude that the doctors and
parents so desperately need.

A child's laugh , lights the country, the world,
our hearts pulling our souls from bouts of
despair

Teenage bands screaming their room down
tight and flush till their red and raw face,
bugging the life from a parents last nerve.

Twenty year olds sigh as their heart is broken
and torn –riiiiiiiip- go the strings that they'd
so readily opened. Halfed in separation,
leaving a little piece -thump, thump ,
thumping - by the hands of their first
palpable love.

A mother's screams as she pushes with love
to rip a new world from the nether to the
world.
Incredible in strength, weaponised sounds to
help produce the coming generations to help
shape our world.

A fathers silence, gripping the room as he
holds back his tears when he holds his new
horns, little murmuring head.

Churchill's quotes, Martin Luther, Miya
Angelou queen of creation and
representation, John Lennon, jfk, George the
poet, Hollie poetry, Shane koyczan... Mr
Nelson Mandela.

The world would be broken, suffering, lost
were it not for the power of our lungs.

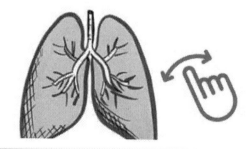

LUNGS
by @beboldtoya

my fragile body survived
as the
ventilator pumped oxygen into
my lungs
I was
in ICU
in a coma
I journeyed as I listened to the faraway chatter
I
was
a prisoner
trapped in my body

  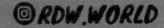

LUNGS
by @poetstale

Lungs

I want to *climb* inside your
lungs and make them function
Press on the dark spots until they're clean and
dry
Show me where to *push*, where to *pump*
I'll live there until the oxygen *flows* smoothly,
until you can *run* down the street effortlessly
Until you can *sing* to us all night
and *dance* till sunrise
p.s.

 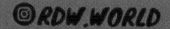

LUNGS
by @ace_of_hearts_ox

Lungs

Not a drop of water in sight,
yet you are drowning.
I turn up the oxygen,
FIFTEEN LITRES AND COUNTING.
EYES OCEAN BLUE,
STARE AT ME, PLEADING,
finger tips turning
THE SAME PALE HUE.
Gasping for breath,
Giving all you have left.
WILLING FOR THOSE LUNGS TO FILL,
Before covid claims another kill.

LUNGS
by @littleblackheartpoetry

LUNGS 2.0

SHE WAS TINY
SHE WAS SMALL
ABOUT TWO AND A HALF
POUNDS IN ALL

ARRIVED WAY BEFORE
HER TIME WAS DUE
FIGHTING FOR LIFE
WAS ALL SHE COULD DO

3 LONG MONTHS
KEPT IN A CLEAR CASE
FOR MOM AND DAD TO SEE
BUT NEVER EMBRACE

GOOD THING SHE'S A FIGHTER
FOR BEING SO YOUNG
SAVED BY HER DOCTOR
AND HER STRONG LITTLE LUNGS

M@littleblackheartpoetry

  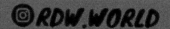

LUNGS
by @the_likwid_lizard

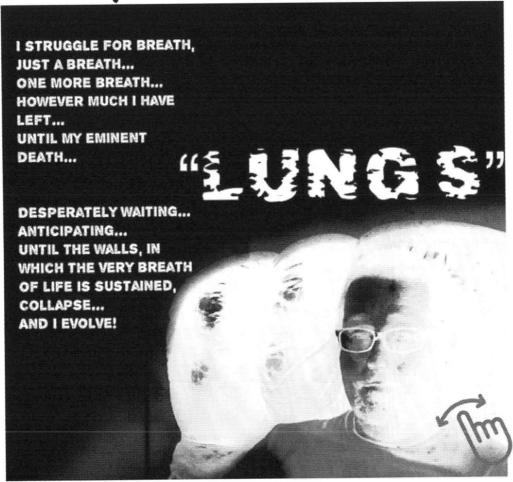

I STRUGGLE FOR BREATH,
JUST A BREATH...
ONE MORE BREATH...
HOWEVER MUCH I HAVE
LEFT...
UNTIL MY EMINENT
DEATH...

"LUNGS"

DESPERATELY WAITING...
ANTICIPATING...
UNTIL THE WALLS, IN
WHICH THE VERY BREATH
OF LIFE IS SUSTAINED,
COLLAPSE...
AND I EVOLVE!

#RDW   WWW.RDW.WORLD   @RDW.WORLD

LUNGS
by @newkirk.jon

Life had magic in it,
        a little stardust,
like I'm a guest
to the rulers of the night.
I watch my chest
laying flat on my back
        in disbelief.
I breathe in and out,
        asking:
"What tells my lungs to breathe?

What connects to this system?

What allows oxygen to bind and move in the
body?"

It's amazing how the breath is,
how it feeds our need for life.
I wonder how deeply we are connected[?]
Exhaling and inhaling,
in with the good, out with the bad,
just passing breath around.

        - - JnNwkrk

LUNGS
by @dr.inkwright

"Lungs"

When I inhale, I prepare to exhale
A simple respiratory norm that typically never fails
Unless I'm snatched up, turn out missing, never to be heard
from again
Or if I'm found in someone's back yard, with no pulse
Obviously I'm out of breath
Or a policeman's pistol is directed at my chest
Investing in humanity seems worthless some days
When you seem to be European prey, because your skin will
antagonize
The racists who cannot face the truth
They're more evil than they verbally are willing to let loose
My lungs are choosing to breathe deeply
Enjoying what is to be cherished
Inhale...
Exhale...I will prevail
"Hey you, hands up"
But officer
"That's enough...hands in the air"
gasp

   – Jose V. Wright, Jr.
     IG @dr.inkwright

LUNGS
by @paulrkohn

As I sink slowly, I hold my breath, brace myself for the pain

when I hit the bottom, aware that the fall will knock the air from my lungs,

from my body,

My heart beat slows, as the last of the air is carried by my blood,

consumed by every extremity of my body in the hope of

keeping me alive.

Hitting the bottom with a thud, I push up, hope to break the surface

before the darkness consumes me, eats me alive. I rise against the pull,

reach for the light.

Gagging, gasping, right before another wave smashes me to the bottom once again.

Paul R Kohn

FOREST

FOREST
by @namans_words

Where once stood deep, dark, dense woods,
now spread there are concrete jungles,
where once the air was fresh and clean,
now breathing there is full of struggles.

Where leaping deers created beaten paths,
now run there miles long tarred highways,
where echoed sounds of screeching and rutting,
now heard are machines' cacophony, nights 'n' days.

Where once freely flourished flora 'n' fauna,
now lie there only a few parks and zoos,
where lived a myriad of rare species,
now found are only homo sapiens on the loose.

On our way from then to now,
we stomped on natural habitats and nests,
by taking the journey from need to greed,
alas! we kept obliterating our forests.

©naman

  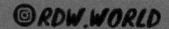

#RDW   WWW.RDW.WORLD   ©RDW.WORLD

FOREST
by @elvisnuke

Forest

Last year's leaves beneath my feet,
sweet smell of damp moss and decay.
Wind whispers secrets through swaying trees
Worn game trails to guide my way.
Some go in, and never come out.
That's the point perhaps.
To get inhaled by the breathing earth,
granted freedom from Time's hard grasp.
Don't come looking. I'm not truly lost.
I know exactly where I am.
A world man hasn't tainted...yet.
How it looked when Life began.

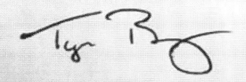 7/13/2020

FOREST
by @juliet_archer

i've laid in the grass
and i've laid in the rain—
the Earth, she knows me well.
yet here i am,
born as i was,
lost in the Forest of Me.

-juliet archer

FOREST
by @wildernest_poetry

take your worn and weary soul
to the forest, dark and dense
feel the earth of scattered leaves,
a thousand years old
touch the plush velvet moss
breathe deeply, the essence
of evergreen and wildflowers
listen to the sounds of wildlife,
birdsong, the scurry of rabbits and deer
look for the bit of light
shining through the canopy above
remember, even in the darkness
there is light, as well
the forest is a healing place
and you are here

FOREST
by @ijameseustice

Through Sassafras and Hemlocks' shade
Passed mossen stones, trunks snaked in vine
Along a thin, foot-beaten path
Descend beneath mens' cog-bound Time
Down steps the looming mountains shed
Tread nimbler by hooves and paws
And talons than by booted feet
Where the air is still, by pollen sweet
Thick with crickets' hymns and flies'
Softens, sweet canopy, green light
To dull Ambitions' bladed thoughts
Where is not Gain or bannered Crime
Where each thing blossoms forth in kind
And takes nor gives more than it needs
Necessity in place of Spite
Where at the bottom of it all
A river bursts forth from the rock
Cascading in a whispered roar
Slow, secret knowledge of the Earth.

FOREST
by @heatherwriting

Forest Song

In my heart I will always be there-
sheltered under your canopy,
breathless and enchanted,
The smell of you still filling my belly
and seeping out of my skin.
You have infused me,
and I am a part of you.
Still floating over your muddy footpaths
Letting winter's soft chill
make snowflakes of my laughter.
If I had known the unbearable expanse of days
that would separate me from you,
I'd have died then on your moss-covered rocks,
Forgetting any other love but yours.

FOREST
by @newkirk.jon

I sat next to a tree in the forest.
Wisely it said, "Feel free to come inside
and delight your heart and explore.
The door is always open."
And like that my soul journeyed inside, and
just like that my spirit transformed.

- - JnNwkrk

  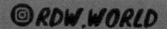

PAKISTAN

Pakistan

For so long, being the victim of brutality,
Citizens are still known for hospitality.

From the dawn, being voice of Kashmir,
Shrieks are suppressed, no one can hear.

Fighting the cursed war, which was imposed,
We bled for others, our blood was disposed.

Being shredded by the poor administration,
Still standing together as a resilient nation.

Founded on the Holy night of Ramadan,
"No power on earth can undo Pakistan" *

 WordsOfAdnan

 #RDW WWW.RDW.WORLD 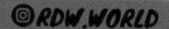 RDW.WORLD

PAKISTAN
by @kuranya_a_poet_dreaming

political differences are dead and buried
as he wipes his sweat-filled brow of concentration
rolling fingers over red leather
opposite eager, nervous darting eyes
and the tap tap tap of willow in the dirt
the only sides that matter here
are batting versus bowling
in the endless summer days
of street cricket
disagreements are few
except between children
who argue over who gets to be
Younis or Ahktar today
innocent children whose dream it is
to make their country proud

©kuranya ~ a poet dreaming ~

PAKISTAN
by @autumnalfyre

Pakistan, you are a mystery,
running half a day ahead of me
on the other side of the world.
Too often if I hear your name
at all, it's associated
with imagined danger,
with invented threats,
with a fear of the unknown
that has clouded our perception
and obscured
your grand mountains,
your vibrant plains,
your people's millions of beating hearts,
hearts like mine.
I want to remove the veil of fear
my country has hidden you behind
and ask you to share
your beautiful secrets with me.

AN
AMERICAN'S
VIEW OF
PAKISTAN

@autumnalfyre

 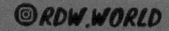

PAKISTAN
by @tharbeland

"Pakistan"

two little birds
flying around in the desert daylight
could not rest
until they found a refuge
away from the war

two little birds
praying that their home be blessed
took with them
a book of many blessings
sometimes if they peered inside
this holy text reminded them to live for
something worth dying for

two little birds
seeking shelter
prayed towards a place called mecca
for one day
their nation would not shed blood anymore
they held hands and spoke words of
wisdom
knowledge of comfort embracing them so

PAKISTAN
by @nasir_beyg

I belong to a country
 Bound by ranges of mountains; in the North
With rivers and plains and plateaus
With deserts and ocean and coasts
With crops and fruit
Where tradition is making way for modernism
And an industry which is striving to stay alive
A country where cricket is almost a religion
And faith in religion is sacred to all
Yet understood and followed in true spirit by very few
Pathans and Balochs; Sindhis and Punjabis
A rainbows of races, ethnicities and casts
Food is spicy yet you would ask for more
We are intelligent and responsible
We are mercurial; we are temperamental
Like a mysterious symphony or an instrumental
Also rich in culture, history and art
We are what you can call a beautiful paradox
We are all this and more; yet one thing we are not
We are not as bad as you are told we are
I would ask you all to visit us once
From Europe or US or Australia or India
And see and judge for yourself
Who we really are
@nasir_beyg

 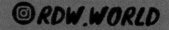

CELEBRATION

CELEBRATION
by @samantha_peterson_poetry

Spring Rain

The aftermath of soggy storms
Drips from effervescent vines
Cerulean wildflowers dance
With each exhale of the wind
Making love to reeds as they sway
Back and forth. Back and forth.
Songbirds harmonize with bullfrogs
Cicadas and katydids
A circused cacophony
Mother Nature's throng of thespians
Synchronizing symphonic notes
Thank Heaven for its tears
Pouring life back in the earth
So each tiny wisp and innocent soul
May celebrate rebirth

- Samantha Peterson

CELEBRATION
by @a.natali.writing

Its a celebration
I'm saying Congratulations
To you and your accomplishments
I always knew you put your heart in this
So today we will be sipping champagne
Dancing all night turning it up to Lil Wayne
We will be taking photos, looking back later
At this life we both chose
You look like your dripping in gold
I like your style, your smile
The way you laugh
Its cute, funny, and uncontrolled
These moments have me flowing
You are the definition of glowing
It's a celebration,
Let's dive into elation
-a. natali

 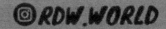

CELEBRATION
by @chrislpoetry

Celebration

Our time here does have a limit

Find a way to enjoy every minute

Everyday should be a celebration

Though for some there's no elation

All of us battling their own demons

One or more, for a million reasons

Peace is the answer, forgiveness is key

You have to let go, to let yourself be

 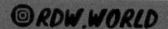

CELEBRATION
by @beboldtoya

Everyday is a CELEBRATION
WHEN I WAKE UP
I am forever thankful for the gift of life
life is not promised
So I value each breath I take
I look forward to experiences
in order to enjoy the peaks
I eat my marshmallows
I dance in the rain
I smile at the blink of an eye
I laugh in the rain
I speak LIFE into me
My LIFE is a MARATHON
Yet I celebrate the short runs/wins
A line might be unrelated but that's the beauty of my life
Sometimes it does not make sense
in the end it ADDS up perfectly to ME
My imperfections are my perfection
My body keeps score
Always celebrating mY Life
Unless you've had a close encounter with MORTALITY
YOU
May never understand
That my Life is a DAILY CELEBRATION

 #RDW    WWW.RDW.WORLD   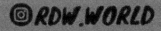 RDW.WORLD

CELEBRATION
by @sonam.wadkar

She celebrated her birth everyday
as her life grew meaningful with need
She celebrated honesty in every word
when truth was a rarity full of deceit
She celebrated her innocence so pure
tainted by the humanity's selfish greed
She celebrated her wisdom unmatched
earned by the pain wrecking her breathe
She celebrated her mind second to none
enticing hearts seeking to fathom her breed
She celebrated her destiny unparalleled
as divinity guided her through the defeat
She celebrated her enduring love endlessly
for untold hearts felt love unbeknownst and free
She celebrated her passionate life for eternity
beyond her ken lived her purpose on a wild spree

- Sonam Wadkar

CELEBRATION
by @sakinas_expressions

Celebrate today,
Tomorrow is no guarantee.
Celebrate moments,
Even the small victory!
Celebrate experiences,
Lessons that failures teach.
Celebrate your own courage
Towards the goals you wish to reach.
Celebrate the love,
Lifelong bonds and freindships!
Celebrate sweet joys
With warm hearts and smiling lips.
Each day is a celebration,
A fresh new beginning,
While the heart beats and limbs move...
Don't fret, keep celebrating!!!!

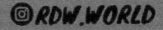

CELEBRATION
by @martindix87

I've written down in my diary that I'm I'm besotted.
I've jotted down on my calendar that I'm addicted.
I have noted down all over my bedroom wall,
how much I miss you.
As if I could forget.
Maybe there is a pattern starting to emerge here.

I am smitten, taken in by your touch.
I am weakened, when you take yourself away.
I have been reading about this in romantic novels.
I should know what happens on the next page.

Tulips are next on my shopping list.
I am forever in disbelief but also scared
that I'm just not good enough.
But every day I grow stronger.

I will wait.
I will wait until I dont need to visit you
and we are together, never to part.

 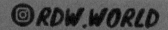

CELEBRATION
by @writenpoetri

when it's love

that happens to you,

you're sucked into a whirlpool,

of recollections and reminders

of your lover, of your untapped feelings.

you see them in everything your eyes rest on,

and a smile graces your lips,

it's a celebration of the radiantly gratifying form,

love comes to you in.

the joy of love's existence;

it's seen,

in the concentration, the new grandmother has

as she knits for her child's child,

resilient fingers weaving tenderness.

it's visible,

in poetry and ; in a photograph,

yet to be written; yet to be clicked.

talking of lovers huddled in a blanket; of friends joking by the lakeside.

it's inescapable, and it comes to you too,

backs you up,

in the corner of your bedroom,

where you sit, trying to shake off the world,

but it comes to you,

and it comes in mirth,

and tells you,

come, it's a celebration of this adjusted reality.

 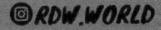

TRAIN
by @danny_boy_poetry

Thoughts are supposed to have a train,
But mine are held in crystal jars,
Attached to zany bumper-cars.
They bounce and bash each other,
As they dance and collide
Across the flaws and walls
Of my tortured old mind.

Occasionally, there's a major crash,
And the thoughts are sent to smash,
Across the crevices and spaces,
And out to the edges,
Of my consciousness.
Waiting for me to pick up the pieces
With uncareful rhyme
And rhythmic glue.

TRAIN
by @thepassivedot

Train

You are like a train
Teasing my body, making your own tracks
Pumping your way through me with your gears
Until you find your destination.
Multiple stops to refuel and offload
Until home-base is reached
Never once do you go off-road.
Steam hissing out at every thrust
Of your engine
Pushing on your immaculate body
Taking me on a journey
I am your railway
I am your passenger
A journey of the century
Just a ticket away.

The Passive Dot

TRAIN
by @caitlinjadepoetry

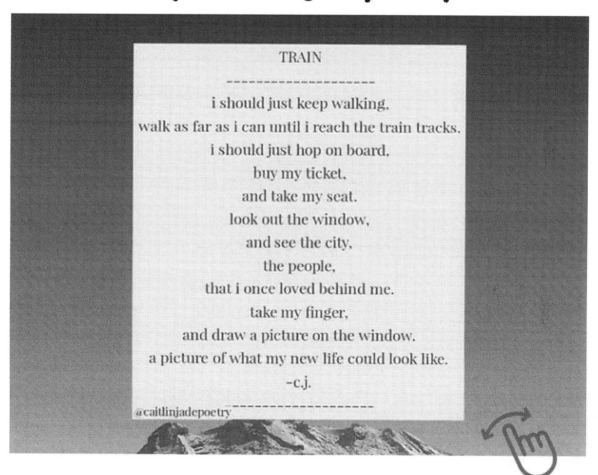

TRAIN

----

i should just keep walking,
walk as far as i can until i reach the train tracks.
i should just hop on board,
buy my ticket,
and take my seat.
look out the window,
and see the city,
the people,
that i once loved behind me.
take my finger,
and draw a picture on the window.
a picture of what my new life could look like.
-c.j.

@caitlinjadepoetry

TRAIN
by @kimberley.poetry

A Cautionary Tale

There's an empty seat
On the train I just missed
It's not a metaphor
But it sort of is

How many trains
Have rolled away from stations
Without me?

How many moments
Have slipped away
Unfelt, unseen?

Something to think about

 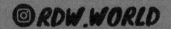

TRAIN
by @lishid619

I tried

Made plans ahead

Ticket at the earliest reserved

To board a train that had already left

My life wasn't mine alone to decide

Did everything for everyone to stay by my side

All I wanted was not to be denied

To board a train that had already left

Things sorted out in nick of time

Rushing to make it before clock chime

If this tension could just sublime

To board a train that had already left

My life never made any demand

Still received a lot of reprimand

All I ever wanted was not for this journey to countermand

To board a train that had already left

Never even booked the first class

Though dreamt of holding that champagne glass

And yell cheers sitting next to a Scottish lass

To board a train that had already left

I know this isn't the last and only train

But only I knew, how it would've been if I had made it

Every single day I wish for a chance

To board that train that had already left

Lishid Mohamed

 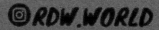

TRAIN
by @pilgrimsofprose

My train of thoughts
Derails each night
When I remember
How our love ran out of steam

We left a trail of carnage
On the tracks
As we walked away
From what could have been

TRAIN
by @_jwritess_

Can you explain?
How to heal this pain,
that's really insane.
How to train my heart and brain!
The only thing that I can't complain,
It's not you or them
It's me,my crowding thoughts
That gaze upon the visionary train,
bell ringing clock ticking...
You'll come again travelling in the lane.
Please explain,what my heart desire
Is all in vain or soon turns to
our old heavenly reign.

Shall I pause it or play it all again?

TRAIN
by @ijameseustice

I waited for you at the station
With my watch and checked it twice,
I tapped the seconds with my shoe
Against the concrete.
A paper blew across the tracks
As the empty tunnel filled with light,
The headline landing at my feet
Said the world was ending.
Your engine squealed against the rails,
I stood and gripped your flowers tighter,
Trying to remember what you looked like.
The thousand faces streaming past
Stared through the glass so strangely back,
The cars stopped, and they rushed out
In a blur of cloudy faces.
I searched the crowd waiting to see you
Beaming through them like a sunray
But it was only ever darkness,
You were only ever expectations,
I never saw you, you never came through,
And the world of course was only, always ending.

@ijameseustice

 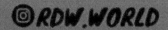

TRAIN
by @kimberley_poetry

A Cautionary Tale

There's an empty seat
On the train I just missed
It's not a metaphor
But it sort of is

How many trains
Have rolled away from stations
Without me?

How many moments
Have slipped away
Unfelt, unseen?

Something to think about

BLOOD

BLOOD
by @saharjaan_

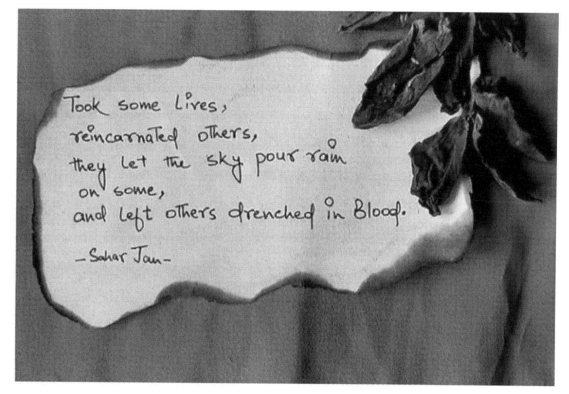

BLOOD
by @poetbythenight

we wear
different skins
different hair
different clothes
even beliefs.
but underneath it all
flows warm blood
and it's the same
for you and me.
it throbs
through all our veins.
we carry it
with all our chains.
red is universal.

BLOOD
by @jbpoetry1

Blood

Warm life-giving blood
gushes from the open wound
like a river of lava
flowing hot and thick,
from the earth's core.
Spurting and frothing with each
desperate breath in and out.
Life fading with every second
as the pulse gets weaker and
the breath becomes more laboured.
The paramedic battles in vain to stem the flow,
but the blade has done its job,
another life taken far too young.

JB

#RDW   WWW.RDW.WORLD   @RDW.WORLD

BLOOD
by @j.wildepoetry

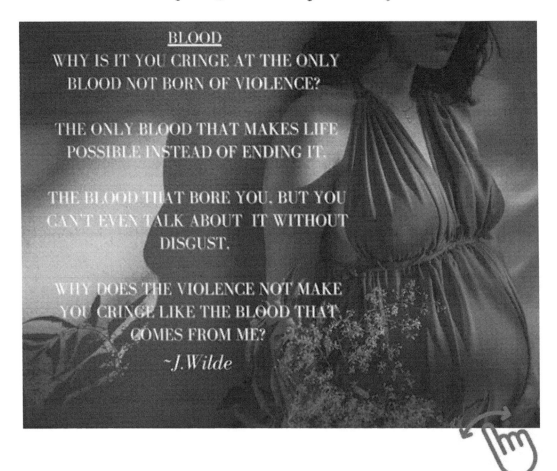

BLOOD

WHY IS IT YOU CRINGE AT THE ONLY
BLOOD NOT BORN OF VIOLENCE?

THE ONLY BLOOD THAT MAKES LIFE
POSSIBLE INSTEAD OF ENDING IT.

THE BLOOD THAT BORE YOU, BUT YOU
CAN'T EVEN TALK ABOUT IT WITHOUT
DISGUST.

WHY DOES THE VIOLENCE NOT MAKE
YOU CRINGE LIKE THE BLOOD THAT
COMES FROM ME?

~J.Wilde

BLOOD
by @pinktypewriterpoems

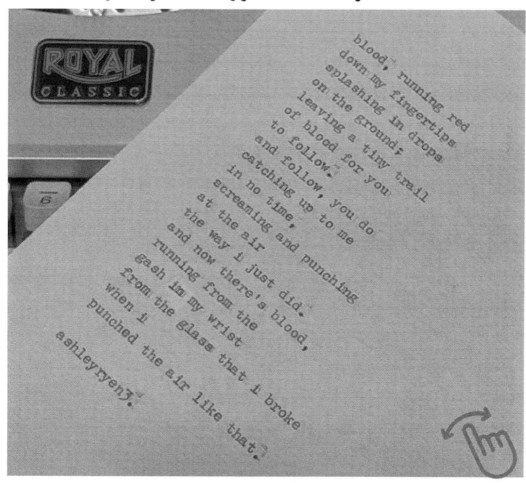

blood, running red
down my fingertips
splashing in drops
on the ground,
leaving a tiny trail
of blood for you
to follow,
and follow, you do
catching up to me
in no time,
screaming and punching
at the air
the way i just did,
and now there's blood,
running from the
gash in my wrist
from the glass that i broke
when i
punched the air like that.

ashleyryen3

BLOOD
by @satwikg_7

Sickening sorrow of the shunned
Boredom at height ut daily tragedy rotund
Contravened the glance of pity mortals
Sans (solace, regard alas chortles)
Cold eerie gust, rush apud visage
Unravels depressing, diables rummage
Dogmas spurn, vindications afloat
Tears churned and bridled smote
Ruthless venture, porous body and soul
Aching for love, inquest me infuse the hole
Blood upon brotherhood, chaos afold
Savagery drive, cut throats tote
Beastly hollers, earth tint crimson
Bequeath the lunar, unholy arisen
Trembling, stifling aether too foul
Dreadful journey, eclipse in deaths cowl
Cordially tarry, for the battle ached
Scorched from placidity, heroes faked
Treachery in Oculi of Father Pax; self cupidity
Man's untold ichor-itch; beastly vile stupidity
panacea for ye malison and plague ?
la réponse est aussi vague....

BLOOD
by @thepassivedot

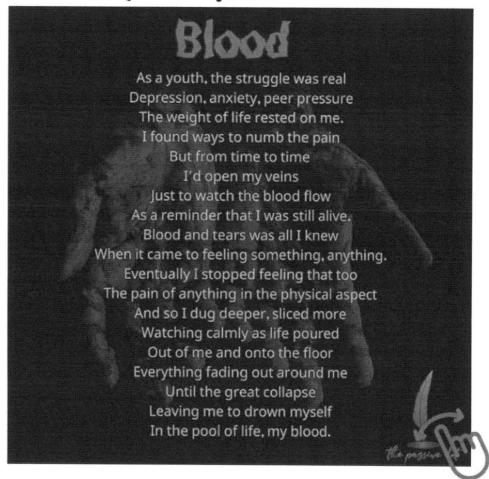

Blood

As a youth, the struggle was real
Depression, anxiety, peer pressure
The weight of life rested on me.
I found ways to numb the pain
But from time to time
I'd open my veins
Just to watch the blood flow
As a reminder that I was still alive.
Blood and tears was all I knew
When it came to feeling something, anything.
Eventually I stopped feeling that too
The pain of anything in the physical aspect
And so I dug deeper, sliced more
Watching calmly as life poured
Out of me and onto the floor
Everything fading out around me
Until the great collapse
Leaving me to drown myself
In the pool of life, my blood.

BLOOD
by @thestoryteller_inc

The blood in my veins pumping at
its pace.
I can feel it all just then,
So loud and clear, intricate
and delicate,
A life-changing thought.
How precious every second is,
I am reminded;
It all came alive as the little strip
dissolved in my tongue.
And suddenly it fades, numbness.

- the Storyteller

@thestoryteller_inc

TEENAGER

TEENAGER
by @kingofthedomain

Angst, pain, sexual confusion, fun and games still
innocent but hidden,
Troubled emotions drowned in hormones
Constant beration by adult morons.
What hellish chance do they have when life is so messy,
the adult berating don't know the damned season, if
their lifetime leaders are so tipsy turvy, what chance
have these children as they mature through puberty.

Life is chaotic, first gasp of air to pushing up daisies, so
why in all hell do we attack our middle grounds. Each of
us are teens one time so why do we forget the crusades
that they fight, to be nice, to be old, to be strong, to get
old, not get stabbed, or have kids, but want sex like a
squid wants ink, they're not wrong, they're just
sometimes lost.

They're the future, so treat them like heroes.

-Grimm

TEENAGER
by @garryrowlands_poet

Back of school
Behind the sheds
With cigarettes
And Playboy magazines.

Drenched
In angst
and teenage rebellion

Lunchtime lovers,
Just turned 13
Tongues entwined
Minds on icecream.
Race
Before the bell for French

Garryrowlands_poet

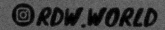

TEENAGER
by @petren33

Just a Teenager
I'm just a teenager,
But everything I do in life seems to be major,
I've been told that what I do now will define what I can do for the rest of my life,
How am I expected to know now what I want to do?
I have no clue,
But I wish I knew what I wanted to do,
It would make life much more simple,
Instead the future just fills me with anxiety.
I want to get by quietly,
But if I do I won't get noticed,
However if I'm loud
I'm told to be quieter.
There is no in between to anything,
I'm either too loud or too quiet,
Happy or depressed,
Know what I want to do or don't have a clue,
In control or in a panic,
Well most of the time
I just feel in a panic,
Or I'm going manic,
Like I could explode,
Go volcanic,
But sometimes
I feel completely in control.
Life gets on top of me sometimes,
But I'm slowly learning how to live.

 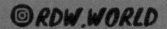

TEENAGER
by @lismcdermott

How do I look?
How do I feel?
Is any of this real?
Worried about my weight,
If I'm going to be late;
"Does this make me look fat?"
"Should you really be wearing that?"
Teachers always asking what I want to be,
Can't they honestly see,
I don't even know myself –
I feel like an unread book on a library shelf.
And why is my friend not talking to me?
Yet is busy squawking
All over Insta about last night?
If my parents hear about that fight,
They'll give me hell,
I might disappear back into my shell.
Being a teen is bad enough,
But social media makes things
100 times more tough.
Can't wait to leave home,
Start travelling far and wide
Making new friends and not feeling alone.

©Lis McDermott 2020

TEENAGER
by @wordsfromtheheart77

Oh the life of a teenager was a struggle some days,

Hormones, boyfriends, and overnight stays.

Arguments with parents and rebellious nights,

Never admitting I was wrong and spouting my rights.

Drinking of alcohol, skipping of school,

Trying my upmost to break every rule.

Now I'm a Mother, I regret my mistakes,

Being a teenager causes heartbreaks.

CMc

TEENAGER
by @sharz_world

Teenager
@sharz_world

Pimples and acne
Laughter and jokes
Fits and rage
Cigarettes and first tokes
Romance and first love
Puberty and stress
Education and studying
Untidy, living in a mess
Arguments and fights
Misunderstandings and confusion
Connections and life long relationships
I'm a teenager in this mixed up fusion

  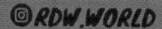

#RDW   WWW.RDW.WORLD   ⓘ RDW.WORLD

TEENAGER
by @danny_boy_poetry

Teenage Dreams

When I was a young wet teen,
My old grandad, rest his soul, said to me,
"Poetry is for puffs and perverts!"

So, I didn't write
Because I thought
he was right,
And poems were wrong,
But now I know
It's wrong for me
not to write.

F&ck you grandad
For the teenage dreams.

SOLDIER

SOLDIER
by @chrislpoetry

SOLDIER ON

All just pawns, yet this is no game

History repeats, more of the same

Battles fought, some land gained

Soldiers lost, the families pained

All this time, we've still to learn

Many more will be sent to burn

@ChrisLpoetry

 #RDW   WWW.RDW.WORLD   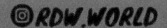 @RDW.WORLD

SOLDIER
by @awaywithwordscal

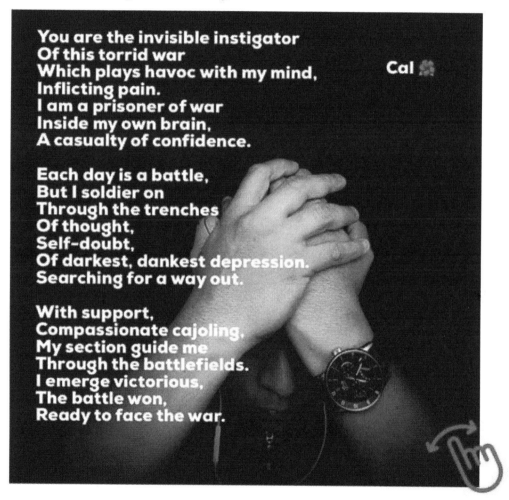

You are the invisible instigator
Of this torrid war
Which plays havoc with my mind,
Inflicting pain.
I am a prisoner of war
Inside my own brain,
A casualty of confidence.

Cal

Each day is a battle,
But I soldier on
Through the trenches
Of thought,
Self-doubt,
Of darkest, dankest depression.
Searching for a way out.

With support,
Compassionate cajoling,
My section guide me
Through the battlefields.
I emerge victorious,
The battle won,
Ready to face the war.

#RDW   WWW.RDW.WORLD   ⊙RDW.WORLD

SOLDIER
by @nasir_beyg

I reincarnate today
As I take birth as a new man
A soldier has hung his boots
Bid farewell to arms
Peeled "Khaki" off his skin
But when you are in it
For as long as thirty years
It's no more a profession
It sinks way deeper
It becomes a part of your soul
It becomes a part of your existence
Inside you never hang your boots
Inside you remain a soldier
Till the day you die
@nasirbaig

  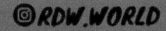

SOLDIER
by @paperbird.me

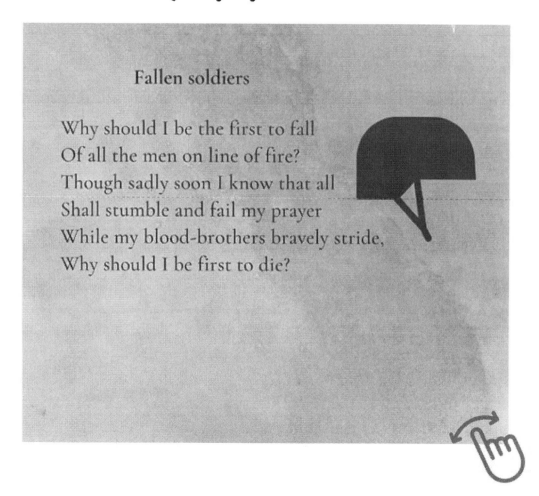

Fallen soldiers

Why should I be the first to fall
Of all the men on line of fire?
Though sadly soon I know that all
Shall stumble and fail my prayer
While my blood-brothers bravely stride,
Why should I be first to die?

SOLDIER
by @poetrybyparkes

Bullets fly overhead
Whistling as they go
Like a murderous orchestra
Performing for the front row
Cowered low
He hides from plain sight
Avoiding the sniper's rifle
Using the cover of the night
He'll move at first light
Once the band stops playing
And move to execute his objective
Amidst all of this slaying
As his comrades kneel praying
Over the top this soldier goes
His fate is now with you dear reader
For it's now only your imagination that knows

SOLDIER
by @nabeel.mohan

One man's soldier is another's terrorist

When I was still a naive bell-end
I made it my personal quest to befriend
a man who's existence I resent.

Brian loves dogs and red-headed women.
Brian fixed planes that dropped bombs on
Yemen.
In Iraq, Brian killed children.
why? I asked, my warmth already spent.

"nine eleven" Brian said.
Today he marches for BLM,
  - forgetting all the dead,
but at least he makes rent.

SOLDIER
by @huwanahoy

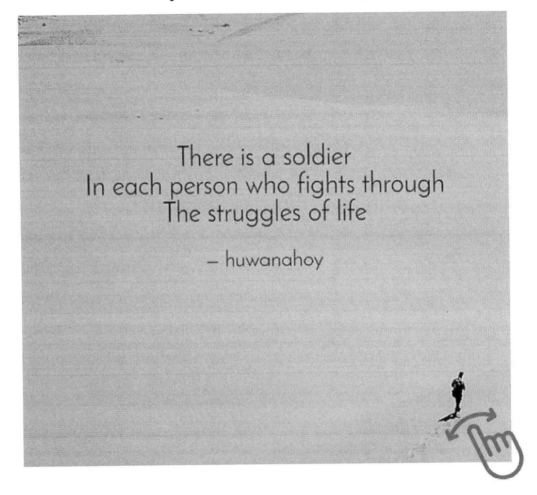

There is a soldier
In each person who fights through
The struggles of life

— huwanahoy

 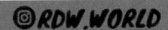

SOLDIER
by @perceived_incriptions

Tiny little soldiers

The march is endless for the little toy soldiers,
All dressed up in their Sunday Finest,
They calmly tell the preacher,
They took a tumble down the stairs,
While they boast bruises of handprints.

Their eyes glaze over accustomed to their pain,
When they go far away from this world,
There is an energy pulling them closer,
Showing them the love they've never known.

Children are like china dolls and they break just as easily,
Like little toy soldiers, they fall in line,
As life is hell for these silent soldiers
That they can go nowhere but up.

They think they have lost their hope on Earth,
But in reality they are just hoping for a better truth.
Tiny little soldiers on their endless march.

-Perceived Incription

SOLDIER
by @thestoryteller_inc

You're a Soldier honey.
Wake up!
Tame the demons, silence the fears, and sharpen
your swords;
Prepare for war!
Oh no, not with them, but this tumultuous battle
within.
Am I good enough?

Nothing can be achieved by staying in.
You with passion brimming in your veins,
Open up.
Tear up the fears that you've bound yourself with
so tightly.
And walk the earth like the warrior you're meant
to be.

Unleash your power.
Lower the ego.
And be an advocate of the light.

- the Storyteller

 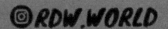

#RDW   WWW.RDW.WORLD   @RDW.WORLD

MOON
by @red.flo_wer

You see, I envy the moon.
She's as free as she's wild.
She outshines even the brightest of stars.
She lights up the dark,
In the way that'd make you think she owned it-
Which she probably did.
She's seen so much and still doesn't crack.
You can tell she's in love with who she is by how
She doesn't mind that her light comes from the sun;
Instead, she sucks it all in and runs wild with it like it's hers.
All those who see her adore her.
She lights the way in the darkest of days and
Remains a constant companion,
To those who are lonely at night.
She's heard so many secrets,
Yet doesn't feel the need to spill.
She dominates the skies alone,
Without feeling the need for a partner.
You see, I envy the moon.

Red_flower

#RDW   WWW.RDW.WORLD   @RDW.WORLD

MOON
by @nasir_beyg

Everytime my heart breaks
I die a little inside
Like a moon diminishing
bit by bit
And I am scared of the
moonless nights
@nasir_beyg

MOON
by @museofdarkness

That night ,
When you sat under the moon,
When your lips first met,
Making your hearts swoon.

When love made itself known,
And your held her hand,
And your shadows made love,
On the cold wet land.

You were still high,
On her breath that day,
When you found me alone
on your way.

You carried her scent,
when you came to me,
And now years later, you say,
It was I that night and not she.

MUSE OF DARKNESS

#RDW   WWW.RDW.WORLD   @RDW.WORLD

MOON
by @j.wildepoetry

You are my sun, I'll be
your moon, and remind
you of how brightly you
can shine in times of
darkness too.

~J. WILDE

MOON
by @nabeel.mohan

I don't worship the sun -
that burning light who promises
eternal life but insists on
heat that leaves you parched,
all his judgement searing, harsh.

I worship the moon
who, in partnership with stars,
gently guides you through the dark.

MOON
by @tash_the_sloth

How must I tell the sun that he died in vain?

Waiting for a love that never came

His fiery fingers reached towards the moon

As her spectral presence danced with the fumes

So close, but never together

Dying each time to catch a glimpse of forever

Their goodbye kiss is painted in the sky

Look up my darling, and open your eyes

~Natasha Huynh

 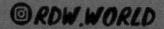

MOON
by @wordsofadnan

Tell me, do I make you smile,
When it's dark and the the sun is down?
When you're carelessly moving around,
Your feet gliding on cold hard ground.
With your hands over your head,
Spinning in circles,
Like you're a moon at its axis.
Tell me, can you see me,
Looking up to you as a source of light?
A guide or just a companion,
Tell me if you feel the same.
Please tell me you're my moon,
Please tell me soon.

WordsOfAdnan

MOON
by @mrchristophersedgwick

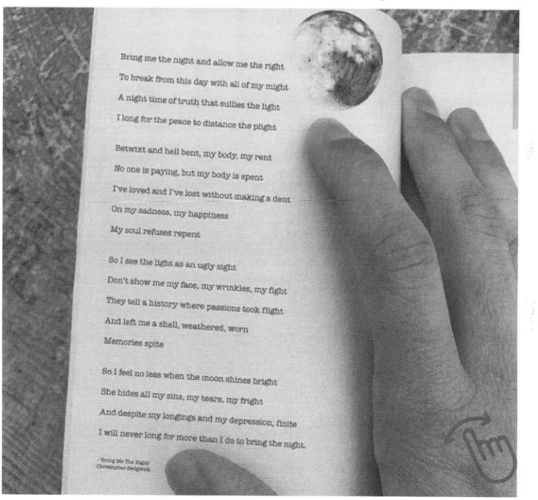

Bring me the night and allow me the right

To break from this day with all of my might

A night time of truth that sullies the light

I long for the peace to distance the plight

Betwixt and hell bent, my body, my rent

No one is paying, but my body is spent

I've loved and I've lost without making a dent

On my sadness, my happiness

My soul refuses repent

So I see the light as an ugly sight

Don't show me my face, my wrinkles, my fight

They tell a history where passions took flight

And left me a shell, weathered, worn

Memories spite

So I feel no less when the moon shines bright

She hides all my sins, my tears, my fright

And despite my longings and my depression, finite

I will never long for more than I do to bring the night.

"Bring Me The Night
Christopher Sedgwick

GHOST
by @whatvasthinks

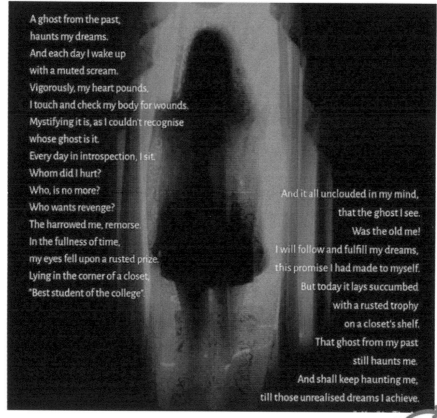

A ghost from the past,
haunts my dreams.
And each day I wake up
with a muted scream.
Vigorously, my heart pounds,
I touch and check my body for wounds.
Mystifying it is, as I couldn't recognise
whose ghost is it.
Every day in introspection, I sit.
Whom did I hurt?
Who, is no more?
Who wants revenge?
The harrowed me, remorse.
In the fullness of time,
my eyes fell upon a rusted prize.
Lying in the corner of a closet,
"Best student of the college"

And it all unclouded in my mind,
that the ghost I see.
Was the old me!
I will follow and fulfill my dreams,
this promise I had made to myself.
But today it lays succumbed
with a rusted trophy
on a closet's shelf.
That ghost from my past
still haunts me.
And shall keep haunting me,
till those unrealised dreams I achieve.

  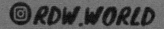

GHOST
by @garryrowlands_poet

In your distance
I hear the
hammering sound
of your silences
hanging in the air
like death,
waiting
in the sidelines
for the ghosts
of you&me

GHOST
by @words_emissions

Grief tore pieces of me
Bit by bit
Until I looked in the mirror
And saw no one
A ghost of myself,
I had become

©words_emissions

GHOST
by @awaywithwordscal

Cal

You're not him;
The man that I remember
Since you left for war
Late last September.
I counted the days,
Oh so many nights,
Dreamed of you
Back home where everything was right.
I see you now,
Slumped at the window
In that old wicker chair;
Staring into your empty whiskey glass
Like you're not really there.
Those haunting eyes
Echo distrust and fear
Every now and again,
They slip a silent tear.
There's no longer any joy,
No more laughter,
We're the personification of disaster.
Fight those flashbacks,
Face your ghosts,
Fight for that man
Who I love the most.

GHOST
by @Melissa.k.c

melissa.k.c | poetry

reminiscent notes
of a desert breeze
floating pale and ghostly
across your heavy eyes
to everyone else
you're but another being
but to me
you're a steady dose
of something bitter sweet
a closed door
selective to open
hesitant to greet
spectacular things
could await us
if you weren't so afraid
just a gifted phobic
destined to destroy
our distant
unknown

GHOST
by @thestoryteller_inc

The scariest are the ones that reside within us,
Reigned by fear, it's deathly rider, smiling like the devil,
Eyes hollow and empty, echoing trenches in our own hearts.
And tonight they go again!
Lights off, darkness pouring in and sleep a distant dream.
They come alive, in a lyric, a movie, a word or whisper.
What we can't control, becomes our deadliest ghost!

  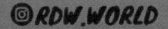

GHOST
by @paulrkohn

When you paint people with the same brush

as those who hurt you in your past

instead of hearing, listening, feeling,

believing in who they truly are,

all you do is break your future;

all you do is resurrect ghosts.

Paul R Kohn

FUTURE
by @heatherwriting

Hereafter

I have painted my future in deep crimson passion
blooming with dahlias
and aubergine splashes of unadulterated joy.
Thick swirls of verdant laughter stand up on the canvas.
I'd make Van Gogh retch with envy
if not for the peaceful hush of this cobalt stream,
Trickling and tripping through twilight-flushed breezes,
Melting sunlight: yellow, orange, red, purple, blue, midnight.
Midnight and stars,
Stars dripping from my hands
Staining me with the light of everything I've ever deserved,
And I have made a new September.

-HK

 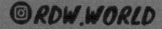

FUTURE
by @kimberley.poetry

FUTURE

I write myself letters
In the form of poems
In past, present and future
tense

Hoping
That at some point across time
Things will line up
And perhaps
One of us
Will make some sense

And we haunt each other
Unable to stand still
All at once
Without will
Under oath
Under cover

 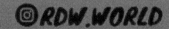

FUTURE
by @Words_filled_with_energy

DEAR FUTURE SELF:

MY FUTURE SELF IS FILLED TO THE BRIM WITH
UNCONDITIONAL LOVE.
IT BEGINS TO OVERFLOW ONTO ALL THE OTHER
BEAUTIFUL SOULS.
IT CAN'T BE CONTAINED AND IT WON'T BE SHUT OFF.
IT SPILLS AND IT DRIPS ALL OVER THE FLOOR.
IT FLOODS THE ROOM WITH UNCONDITIONAL LOVE.

-Me

FUTURE
by @beboldtoya

I cheated on
PAST with PRESENT
eventually I broke it off
with
PAST
to explore my options with
PRESENT
soon PRESENT
caught me frolicking with
FUTURE
he labeled me a cheater
I didn't mind
because my
FUTURE seemed brighter
with
FUTURE

  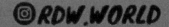

#RDW WWW.RDW.WORLD @RDW.WORLD

FUTURE
by @neelofer_nova

The future
by nature
is unknown.
We predict, guess and hope.
We plan and stress.
We decide what the future looks
like, you and me.
Tomorrow is a new day, they say
And so is the day after that
But if the future depended on
yesterday
Would you hold any regrets?

@NEELOFER_NOVA

FUTURE
by @wordsfromtheheart77

Future

Her hands poised over the crystal ball, she glared intensely at me,

'Relax, my dear, sit back, enjoy. Let me tell you what I can see'.

Gazing into the colourful sphere, her words began to spill,

Listening intently to my future, all was well.. until..

Her voice began to tremble and she cut the reading short,

She said she wasn't feeling well, she was going to abort.

I left the building feeling strange, like something wasn't right,

Pain in my chest, fall to the ground, I head towards the light...

CMc

FUTURE
by @emaraising1

FUTURE...

I don't know what the future holds,
but for now....
I have you to talk to.
I have you who makes me happy.
I have you who makes me laugh.
I don't need much.
You say:"One day at a time."
And this is all that matters to me..
I try.
We try.
We accept what is. Now.
One day at a time,
I don't want to think about the
future.
We are here. Now.
The best is yet to come.

By emaraising1

FUTURE
by @_juliasko

Breath of a distant sea
Heave of a fallen breeze
Future is your given name

Your puff distorts all truth
Creates all prolonged thought
A series of mysteries

Future you perplex us
Your air a humid plague
Unbreathable yet aware

Who is Future?
By Julia Skoczypiec

BIRTHDAY

BIRTHDAY
by @awaywithwordscal

Another year,
Another glass raised,
Another heartfelt speech,
Another opportunity to
remember you.
I wish you were still here
Still dancing your silly dance moves,
Still singing your gorgeous heart out,
Still sharing your glitter with
the world.
The happy girl in red
Taken from us far too soon.
My girl.
My friend.
Happy birthday.

Cal

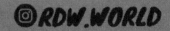

BIRTHDAY
by @autumnalfyre

MILESTONES

Hurry up, you're getting old
Since I was a kid, this is what I've been told
Blow out the candles and make a wish
On my birthday, I write a list
As if I'm supposed to make a report
To prove in some ways I don't fall short
All those milestones I should have reached:

    Have you tasted first love? Isn't it sweet?

    You don't know how to drive? How can you survive?

    Aren't you done with college yet? If it were me, I'd be upset.

    Don't you have a career? Have you checked the year?

    If by now you haven't bought a home

    You'll die before you pay off that loan

    So many countries you should have visited

    Don't you realize your time is limited?

I look to the future with goals in mind
I equate birthdays with arbitrary deadlines
This year I turned thirty-one
How much more should I have done?

BIRTHDAY
by @newkirk.jon

I hear the morning might warm up.
What a gift when you're freezing,
it makes you wonder.

The grandchild smiles like summer
flowers still extending a hand in the
dead of winter.

How we speak for the weekend to
celebrate,
but what for?

We warm up our frosty car,
filling the snow dust air with exhaust
making new tire tracks to the store.

In the depths of winter we ordered a
layered cake to celebrate another snow
covered birthday,

but what am I, but another cold winter
day.

            - - JnNwkrk

BIRTHDAY
by @samantha_peterson_poetry

Birthday

On the day you were born,

Heaven bent down and kissed the earth

She cupped it in her hands

Gently rocking the oceans to sleep

Beneath blue black moon glow

Sang melodies that brought the skies to tears

Love rained from the atmosphere

Pooling around blistered, calloused toes

Life bloomed from dampened stones

And peace fell over our souls

Then she smiled a knowing smile

For the beautiful imprint she left on the world

- Samantha Peterson

BIRTHDAY
by @_ashley_words

Lost joys of birthdays

Balloons, fairy lights
dresses so bright
once young, it all felt so right
happy faces and smiles around worth a sight
we laugh, dance and eat the whole night
with family and friends, a day full of delights
Then life happened and I grew up to fight
my battles and all the plights
birthdays became more of a dull sight
just another day for my pains to hide
miseries of life alight
filling my soul with fright
but wish for my birthday joys to return aright
for I break down at times in contrite
oh how badly I want to requite
all the love being showered and be alright
for I want to dawn upon me, the light
take away all my pains in slight
towards happiness I want to be guide
to again be a part of all the birthday delights,
balloons and fairy lights
wearing dresses so bright
for things to feel once again alright.

– Ashleywords

WHITE
by @nilofer_taj

Why do I always remember
my dreams in glaring white? -

Sun-flushed tulips
shedding their crimson in frenzied haste
at the gentlest stroke of my fingers?

Raging blue waves
fading into an eerie milkiness
as they lash at my trembling feet?

And you,
a long-lost treasure,
a ghastly white shadow,
staring at me through those glass walls
I crumbled trying to tear down!

- nilofertaj

 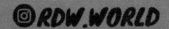

WHITE
by @caitlinjadepoetry

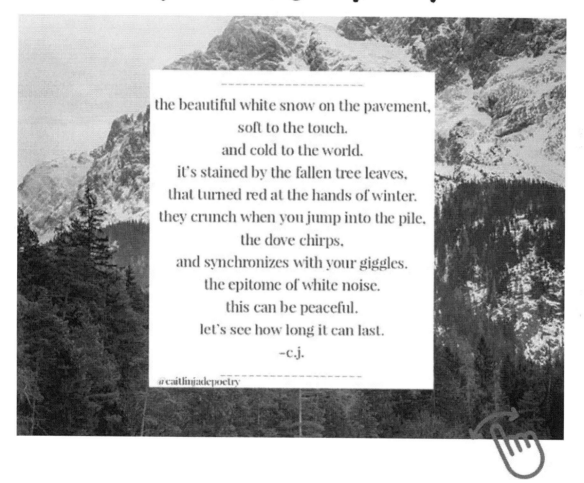

the beautiful white snow on the pavement,
soft to the touch.
and cold to the world.
it's stained by the fallen tree leaves,
that turned red at the hands of winter.
they crunch when you jump into the pile,
the dove chirps,
and synchronizes with your giggles.
the epitome of white noise.
this can be peaceful.
let's see how long it can last.

–c.j.

@caitlinjadepoetry

WHITE
by @namans_words

The colour of fresh snow,
and flagbearer of everything
illuminous,
incandescent, and
immaculate,
stands helplessly
manipulated,
messed-up, and
maligned by a
mindless few.

'White' is crying for rescue
from the dark abyss
it's been pushed into,
for ages.
If it represents
what white-skinned say it does,
it would rather be called
anything but 'White' !

©naman

WHITE
by @lismcdermott

WHITE

Being white means –
Never thinking twice about where you travel in the world,
Never systematically having racist abuse into your face
                                hurled.
Never having to change your name when looking for work,
Never being stopped and searched regularly, by a law gone
                                berserk.
Never being judged on your intelligence by the colour of
                                your skin,
Never having to worry about entry to anywhere; you'll
                                always get in.

The way we live our lives is unlimited –
The true meaning of white privilege.

© Lis McDermott 2020

WHITE
by @secretwriter1427

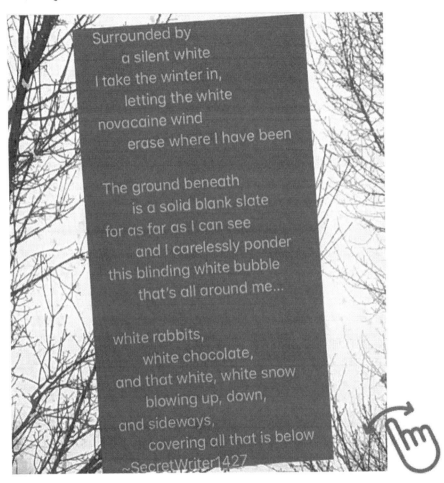

Surrounded by
a silent white
I take the winter in,
letting the white
novacaine wind
erase where I have been

The ground beneath
is a solid blank slate
for as far as I can see
and I carelessly ponder
this blinding white bubble
that's all around me...

white rabbits,
white chocolate,
and that white, white snow
blowing up, down,
and sideways,
covering all that is below
~SecretWriter1427

 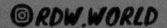

WHITE
by @wildernest_poetry

COCO

my little white cat, Coco,
she's an angel, she's a devil
in her defense she was feral,
in her prior life, she had to be tough
at the shelter, I held her on my lap,
she purred, I said "I'll take her"
I was told I could bring her back
(return her?) anytime, as she was
a "mean girl" mean?
fear can appear as mean
I never saw that side of her,
until I took her to the vet,
she growled
so ferociously
they didn't
want to
see her
ever
again

then,
there was
the time
at the
DC airport
when she
nearly gave
a TSA agent
a heart attack
...there was blood
I was told "that cat would
not be boarding a plane"
so we went went home
I flew out the next day,
alone
I think, in a way,
we're just two
lonely rejects
destined to
give each other
love and comfort
in a fierce world

@wildernest_poetry

WHITE
by @thepassivedot

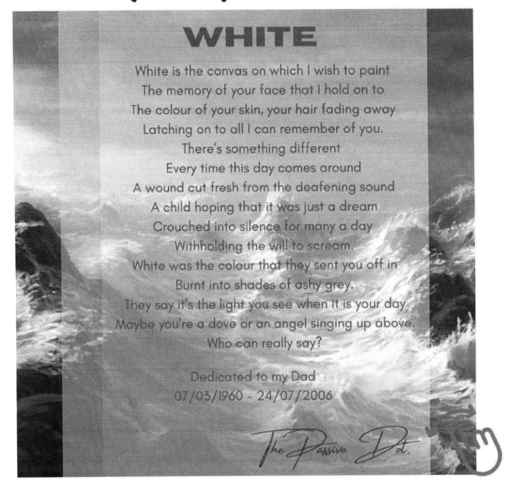

WHITE

White is the canvas on which I wish to paint
The memory of your face that I hold on to
The colour of your skin, your hair fading away
Latching on to all I can remember of you.
There's something different
Every time this day comes around
A wound cut fresh from the deafening sound
A child hoping that it was just a dream
Crouched into silence for many a day
Withholding the will to scream.
White was the colour that they sent you off in
Burnt into shades of ashy grey.
They say it's the light you see when it is your day.
Maybe you're a dove or an angel singing up above.
Who can really say?

Dedicated to my Dad
07/03/1960 - 24/07/2006

The Passive Dot.

#RDW WWW.RDW.WORLD ◉ RDW.WORLD

WHITE
by @_ashley_words

Whites

Aren't we all given a white canvas
to paint our lives whichever way we want
then why do we complain it was destined to be
a burnt black or bleed in red
we could have kept it as fair and unmessed
as the white winter snows or the white lilies
that stands out amongst the coloured beds
of roses, sunflowers and marigolds.
White comes as an escape to me from
the thick layers of plastic crayons
on my canvas
which all seems like absurd
and confused and rattling
and white sneaks in as a pause,
as a moment of pacific and tranquil
that leaves with solidity to get through the coloured days
Aren't white beautiful in itself
colourless yet coloured, pure and calm
apart from the chaos it brings to races at times,
it does fine as a colour to stand between
as a symbol of peace and eternal harmony
as a symbol of prosperity in silence
as a symbol of love in the insurgencies
for I sometimes wish the colour of love
be white and wonder will it hurt any less.

@iam_bhargbhi

WHITE
by @edgeofpoetry

white noise

streetlights burn/branding themselves
onto my skin/so i will always belong
to this place/it is a claim i can't
escape/so i speak in fake accents/and
walk differently/but i am the white
noise/in your head/and mine/i turn up
the volume/i don't want to hear what
i'm thinking/

i look in fun house mirrors to see
myself clearly/and look inside myself/
there are matches burning holes in my
pockets/and i am an overdue book/
burning a hole in my bag/i am turning
up the volume/but/i can't tell if this
is white noise/or/just noise/

7/24/20
kim escobar

NIGHTCLUB

NIGHTCLUB
by @nasir_beyg

Nightclubs to me are like
cemeteries
Where bodies alive drink
and dance
Till they feel as dead as the
souls inside
@nasir_beyg

NIGHTCLUB
by @alps.pen

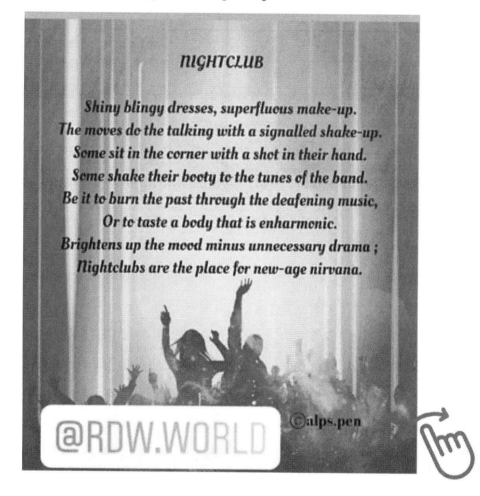

NIGHTCLUB

Shiny blingy dresses, superfluous make-up.
The moves do the talking with a signalled shake-up.
Some sit in the corner with a shot in their hand.
Some shake their booty to the tunes of the band.
Be it to burn the past through the deafening music,
Or to taste a body that is enharmonic.
Brightens up the mood minus unnecessary drama ;
Nightclubs are the place for new-age nirvana.

@RDW.WORLD

©alps.pen

#RDW   WWW.RDW.WORLD   @RDW.WORLD

NIGHTCLUB
by @rupa_reflects

HER NIGHTCLUB JAUNTS

You get what you can
She gets what she wants
She dances with another now
On her weekend nightclub jaunts
'Sweetheart, Love, My Baby'
You called her by those names
Too bad she found out
All your tricks and games
Unwary, you gave someone
A reason to make her smile
You might not regret this
But it will take you a while
To know you lost the moon
As you chased the glittering stars
You may lament or sway
Your blues away in disco bars

Rupa Verma Sanan

 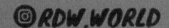

#RDW   WWW.RDW.WORLD   @RDW.WORLD

NIGHTCLUB
by @wildernest_poetry

RDW's Poet's Prompt Nightclub
we don't need a neon sign to find the place,
there's always a poet tending bar
around the clock, all time zones,
it's a poet party, around the world
no need to be alone, there's always a chair for you
dressed to the nines or in your pjs, it's all just fine
bring your good cheer, we'll all have a beer or two,
bring your sorrows, there's single malt Scotch whiskey
for your tears, dear muse
we will write poems for you, just to make you laugh
and pick up the pieces of you
we pen words of love and joy, hope and heartbreak,
the beauty of nature,
the great lost and found of the universe
and all the evil and injustice which makes us scream!
we'll recite our club poems
in those oh, so smooth mellifluous voices
and make everything alright, at least for a little bit
so, have a seat, get comfortable
and pray tell, what will it be for you this evening?
poetry or prose?

@wildernest_poetry, on behalf of the RDW Poetry Collective

NIGHTCLUB
by @patriciahelenwriter

NIGHTCLUB

As night descends
Small groups of friends
All dressed in garb so fine
Meet downtown and get in line
Hearts beat to the throb of nightclub pulse
Heady anticipation felt is something else
Live band music or DJ's platter picks
Promise freeing surge of adrenalin fix
Sexed up vibes with flow of booze
At bar and dance floor players' move
Inhibitions are lost inside the club
Raw and alive in hive of nightclub hub

  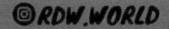

NIGHTCLUB
by @jbpoetry1

Nightclub

hot sweaty and dark
bodies gyrating to noise
morning after pill

JB

NIGHTCLUB
by @fromthehearts_poetsunited

Recalling the day we last met,
Everything around was
so cool and wet.
That Nightclub was at
its all-time best.
Your nasty smile was
difficult to neglect.
The last time I felt you
around my neck.
Your arms on my waist
was a lovely heck.
That amazing evening
on the rocking deck.
I swear, I will never forget!

—NS

DANCE
by @samyukta_81d

Why does she dance to the
morning birdsong
gracefully gliding through
the embers of dawn?
She's a sight to see, her
movements sublime,
an eternal symphony
inside her head

dewdrops on her lashes
grass between her toes
to move
to escape
to set herself free. ~Asta

DANCE
by @beboldtoya

moving my body is necessary
so I enjoy dancing
sometimes
I dance
until I am wet
I love it when the sweat
meets my brows
drips down my
lips and steal a kiss
its even better when
when I slow things down with
a partner
and our cheeks
are pressed up against each other
we get lost in the rhythm of each other
I love to dance
partner or Not

 #RDW   WWW.RDW.WORLD   @RDW.WORLD

DANCE
by @emmarosehope

Dancing to my silly music,
He doesn't dance, so a treat for me
Placing a kiss, so blissfully on my
forehead
And strokes my hair so gently
Tugging it to lift my head up and
reach my lips
Looking deep into my soul
Leaning his head, his lips on mine
Possessing each other, whole

DANCE
by @wildernest_poetry

tango
cuts deep
laser sharp

steady the hand
which holds the flame
hide the tremble

quiet the heart
hear the music
feel the passion
be the rhythm

such is the tango
this seductively
dangerous
lover's dance

@wildernest_poetry

DANCE
by @fifleuriepoetry

Under gold lights that gleam,
A disco ball glitters and glows,
Lost in a trance of time,
To the music we sway so slow.

Our faces beaming with hopes,
What a life we were about to start,
Our smiles glint off the mirrors,
In your hands you held my heart.

Now your daughter dances,
Under silver ball wedding rays,
Your voice sifts softly on song,
Echoes what you'd have wanted to say.

But I'm here. Surrounded by love,
From the beautiful bounty we grew,
Now shadows through shimmers peep,
The shine of life dimmed without you.

Fifleuriepoetry

 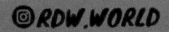

DANCE
by @whatvasthinks

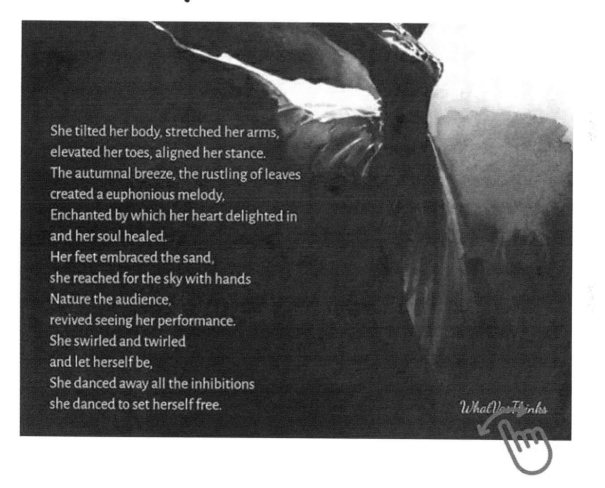

She tilted her body, stretched her arms,
elevated her toes, aligned her stance.
The autumnal breeze, the rustling of leaves
created a euphonious melody,
Enchanted by which her heart delighted in
and her soul healed.
Her feet embraced the sand,
she reached for the sky with hands
Nature the audience,
revived seeing her performance.
She swirled and twirled
and let herself be,
She danced away all the inhibitions
she danced to set herself free.

WhatVasThinks

#RDW   WWW.RDW.WORLD   @RDW.WORLD

DANCE
by @nasir_beyg

Dance of the dying
The legend goes that there was a king who would make his slaves dance to the drum beats. Slaves would be following specific dance routine of repeated steps and when they would have been dancing for a while, he would ask the executioner to chop off their heads and place hot metallic plates to seal their necks. Their nervous system would still keep them dancing till they collapsed. This was called, "dance of the dying".
The tradition goes on in the modern world as most of us still keep dancing despite having been dead inside. Without even knowing or wanting to. Drums keep beating, we keep following the routine and no one can tell. The period however varies, ranging from a few years to decades and for a few it lasts a lifetime.
@nasir_beyg

BUS
by @namans_words

THE LAST BUS

WHILE YOU CAN, DO GET LATE
AND MISS A FEW BUS RIDES.
RUN BEHIND TO CATCH A FEW,
AND HANG ONTO THEIR SIDES.
EXPERIENCE THE LONG QUEUES
AND EVER-RUSHING CROWDS -
SWEATING AND SMELLING,
PUSHING AND PULLING,
BITCHING ABOUT THEIR NEIGHBOURS,
SOME DRUNKEN, SOME SOBER.

RELISH NUMEROUS BUMPY RIDES,
BEFORE IT ALL SLOWS DOWN
AS WE NEAR OUR STOP.
THEN, HOWEVER MUCH YOU WANT,
YOU WON'T BE ABLE TO
ENJOY ALL THESE FUSS.
WHEN IT COMES
TO TAKE YOU ONTO
JOURNEY BEYOND THE CLOUDS,
IT WON'T MISS TO PICK YOU UP -
THE INEVITABLE LAST BUS!

©naman

 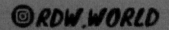

BUS
by @alps.pen

A queue waited for the bus.
There was chaos and fuss.
Their perfumes met and did the talking.
Nice taste, erotically stimulating!
On boarding the bus, she saw him and smiled
His heart skipped a beat, like a little child.
Hope soared high amidst glare and frown
as they both headed to the downtown.
Castles were built with exclusive crowns.
His queen was draped in a silken gown.
He fumbled in his head to speak out his heart
Woof! She had already disappeared at the Mart.
What could have lasted enormous rough tides,
an introvert's love-story ended with a bus ride!

==x==

©alps.pen

 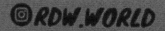

BUS
by @nabeel.mohan

They'd turned it into a place to eat!
No window panes and
they'd torn out the old seats,
lining either side
with chairs and tables, the kind
that look like bars.
That's were we sat with our
backpacks between our knees,
barely awake but still
salivating to sizzling meat.
The floors fondly kept
their quintessential grime
and I'm happy to report
that this time, they'd parked in a field.

Because I'm sure you'll agree
there's nothing quite like eating
a hot English breakfast
to the bleating of sheep.

BUS
by @samantha_peterson_poetry

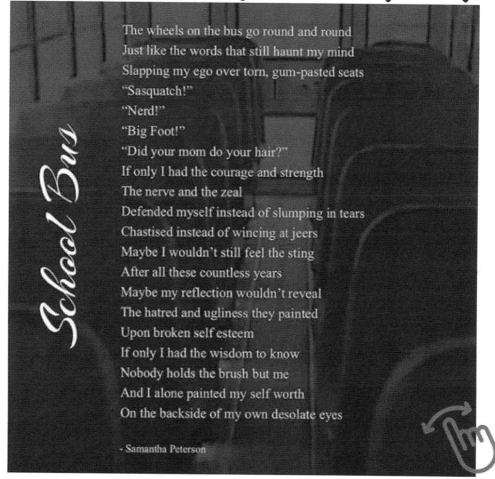

School Bus

The wheels on the bus go round and round
Just like the words that still haunt my mind
Slapping my ego over torn, gum-pasted seats
"Sasquatch!"
"Nerd!"
"Big Foot!"
"Did your mom do your hair?"
If only I had the courage and strength
The nerve and the zeal
Defended myself instead of slumping in tears
Chastised instead of wincing at jeers
Maybe I wouldn't still feel the sting
After all these countless years
Maybe my reflection wouldn't reveal
The hatred and ugliness they painted
Upon broken self esteem
If only I had the wisdom to know
Nobody holds the brush but me
And I alone painted my self worth
On the backside of my own desolate eyes

- Samantha Peterson

LIPSTICK
by @littleblackheartpoetry

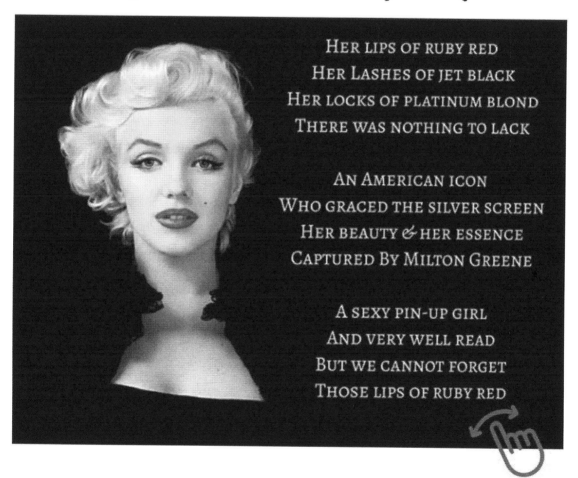

HER LIPS OF RUBY RED
HER LASHES OF JET BLACK
HER LOCKS OF PLATINUM BLOND
THERE WAS NOTHING TO LACK

AN AMERICAN ICON
WHO GRACED THE SILVER SCREEN
HER BEAUTY & HER ESSENCE
CAPTURED BY MILTON GREENE

A SEXY PIN-UP GIRL
AND VERY WELL READ
BUT WE CANNOT FORGET
THOSE LIPS OF RUBY RED

LIPSTICK
by @patriciahelenwriter

LIPSTICK

Moist strokes
Paint oil-oozing pigments
Of claret reds and raisin browns
Corals and pinks and fleshy-nudes
Across a canvas of colourless lips
Palettes of sensual colour roll lavishly
In jojoba and cocoa butter emollients
Thick and sticky carnauba wax smoothed
To deepen matte stained seductive lips
Drawing attention to a beautiful mouth
Hungry to be kissed

LIPSTICK
by @autumnalfyre

LIPSTICK

Never bold enough for lipstick until I was about twenty-five,
traveling for a wedding, I'd forgotten my clear gloss at home
Walk to the drugstore by the hotel
buzzing with a few glasses of wine
I picked out the first shade I found
the color of a child's red crayon
A groomsman pulled me onto the dancefloor
and twirled me around as my relatives
watched from the edges and filmed it
"We had no idea you could dance like that"
There's a lot you don't know about me
I tried to paint those secrets on back home
let a few more of my colors show but it was never the same
"Are you wearing lipstick? Who are you trying to impress?"
My boldness met with sneering questions
like a mother's spit-wet thumb to rub my smile away
Sometimes a loud color draws attention better than loud words,
and my words are never loud
Come closer and listen

@autumnalfyre

LIPSTICK
by @caitlinjadepoetry

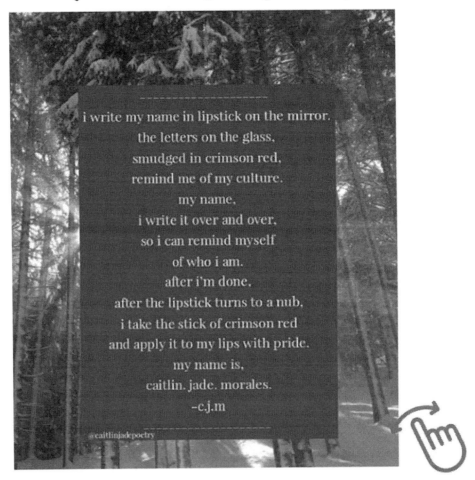

i write my name in lipstick on the mirror.
the letters on the glass,
smudged in crimson red,
remind me of my culture.
my name,
i write it over and over,
so i can remind myself
of who i am.
after i'm done,
after the lipstick turns to a nub,
i take the stick of crimson red
and apply it to my lips with pride.
my name is,
caitlin. jade. morales.

–c.j.m

@caitlinjadepoetry

LIPSTICK
by @s.i.m.true

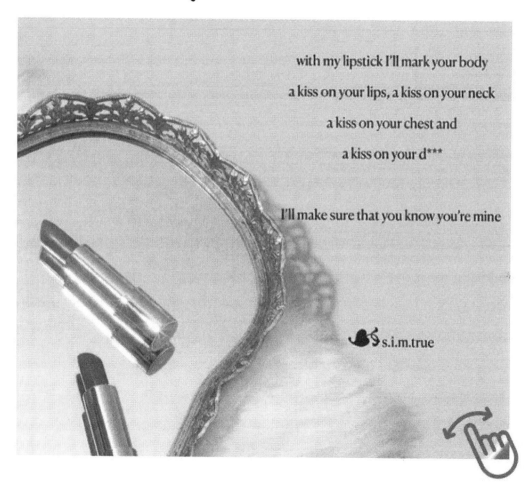

with my lipstick I'll mark your body

a kiss on your lips, a kiss on your neck

a kiss on your chest and

a kiss on your d***

I'll make sure that you know you're mine

s.i.m.true

LIPSTICK
by @nabeel.mohan

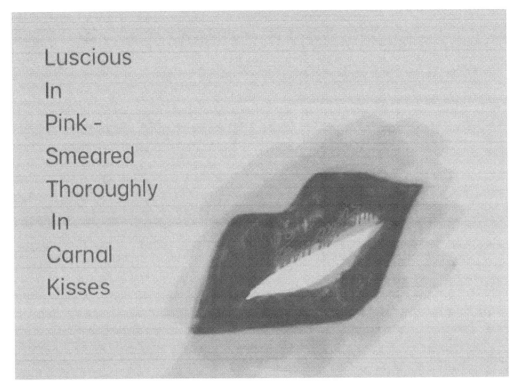

Luscious
In
Pink -
Smeared
Thoroughly
In
Carnal
Kisses

LIPSTICK
by @melissa.k.c

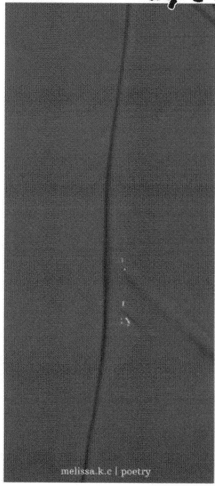

melissa.k.c | poetry

Lipstick
On foggy mirrors
Water over smeared eyes
The woman takes a bow
At the drain that's
Become her life
Relating
Debating
Brawling with the inner
Demons she holds inside
Subdued by immediate
Pleasures
Pressured to keep it
All together
Lipstick
On foggy mirrors
And love letters
Drawn in the sand

 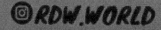

CASTLE
by @aniakiplan.writer

I need no castle
To entertain the masses
My reign is filled
With focus
On a stronghold
That needs no brick
To be a fortress

CASTLE
by @nasir_beyg

You made me
A castle of white sand shining
Gave me a heart of gold
And pearls to ornate my soul
On the shore of a heartless sea; with waves vicious and mad
Ruthless and relentless
Breking my heart; tearing my soul
Knocking down my walls; reducing me back to a lump of sand
Moonless nights prayed; in silence black and dark
A blessing you bestowed
A mermaid lost her way and landed on the shore
Her eyes brown and big; her lips lucius red
Her bosom firm; filled with potion of warmth and love
Her hands shaped me up; into a castle again
Kissing my heart and soul; taking away the pain
In her locks curled and dark; keeping me safe from waves insane;
With no lives without each other
Knowing we are forever
But in her heart dwells a notion
She has a castle where she can never live and I know she belongs to the ocean
nasir_beyg

CASTLE
by @museofdarkness

To unbreak my heart, I needed some magic.
 I sang many songs and danced many dances.
I wrote many words and read many books.
I tried all the wild flowers and fragrances
 in all the wild woods.

None of it worked.

Then I gathered all the stones,
That were hurled at my heart
And built my castle with them.
I gathered all my demons and all my monsters
And the fairies and the angels too,
I, the mistress of them all,
I, the queen of my stone castle.
And I summoned my powers and turned into a witch
Who would cook up hearts, till they were tender and done
And would eat them up to strengthen my own.

MUSE OF DARKNESS

CASTLE
by @growfreepoetry

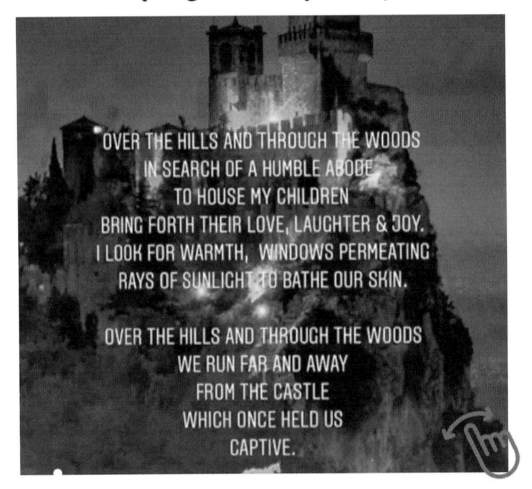

OVER THE HILLS AND THROUGH THE WOODS
IN SEARCH OF A HUMBLE ABODE
TO HOUSE MY CHILDREN
BRING FORTH THEIR LOVE, LAUGHTER & JOY.
I LOOK FOR WARMTH, WINDOWS PERMEATING
RAYS OF SUNLIGHT TO BATHE OUR SKIN.

OVER THE HILLS AND THROUGH THE WOODS
WE RUN FAR AND AWAY
FROM THE CASTLE
WHICH ONCE HELD US
CAPTIVE.

CASTLE
by @a.natali.writing

In my castle, I am free, roaming where I please.
Paintings, sculptures, and tapestries drive me to my humbled knees.
Stonewalls with stained glass windows, peaking pinnacles, strike through to the heavens.
A room for solitude. Where I can express my gratitude, contemplate my thoughts, and lessons.
Cabinets flooded with books, a student I am first, a legend in the making, my truth will be told.
Fire illuminates my path, through to secret chambers filled with treasures, riches, and gold.
Our jeweled copper chalices overflow with wine, beer, and mine with mead.
Iron tables, topped with grapes, hen, and bread. Nearby, a spiced digestive.
Strings echo in the hall, lyres, and harps. Ethereal voices speak with insistence.
Poetically, magically, and romantically. Declaring our future into existence.
In the tower keep, is where I go to flee from the revenants of the night.
Veiled in a black hooded cloak, fearless, starring out into the moonlight.
Walking in sand, feeling the warmth, I am grateful to be flesh and bone.
I will forever be a King of my man-made castle and a ruler of my throne.
-a. natali

CASTLE
by @1poetickathryn

I will build you a castle
With my two bare hands
Announce to other kingdoms
In faraway lands
Present you the key
Crown you my king
You shall become my everything
Your every wish
Is my command
It would be an honor
If you would
Take my hand
You are my person
Until the end
The day that I found you
My life truly began

  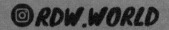

#RDW   WWW.RDW.WORLD   @RDW.WORLD

CASTLE
by @poetry_dove

We're building sand castles
On the beach
You reach to grab my
hand
That look, your eyes
Pure love
Unsanitized

  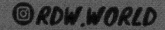

#RDW   WWW.RDW.WORLD   ©RDW.WORLD

CASTLE
by @alexjonaswrites

I built you a castle
with a view of the sea
but we couldn't survive
the waves

CASTLE
by @autumnalfyre

CASTLE

I have built stone walls around me
I am queen of my own castle
Rarely venturing outside
Since it's such a hassle
To let down that drawbridge
And walk around unprotected
As delicate as a wallflower
Pretending I'm not so easily affected
By being forgotten and never
Being the one he holds closest
So I fade away like a ghost
That no one noticed
And return to haunt these cold halls
Of this fortress I call home
I am secure and shielded here
But I'm so tired of being alone

@autumnalfyre

SCOTLAND

SCOTLAND
by @wordsfromtheheart77

Scotland

Scotland, my country, my beautiful home,

Where fields are green and the Highland cows roam.

The people are friendly, they like a good drink,

They'll greet you with handshakes, smiles and a wink.

Irn bru, haggis, their sausages are square,

There's many a strange thing for offer up there.

With views stretching out the length you can see,

There's no place in the world, that I'd rather be.

CMc

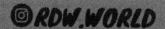

 **#RDW** **WWW.RDW.WORLD** **@RDW.WORLD**

SCOTLAND
by @jbpoetry1

Nessie

in the deep dark depths
monstrous mysteries abound
luring the hopeful

JB

  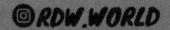

SCOTLAND
by @kingofthedomain

Failte a chairaid to my tale of the Scots.

From the highland and hills to our cities so cold,
The Scots are a people so ancient and bold,
Old lads are so cheeky, they may make you blush
And oor ladies so gorgeous with hair red as pure lust.

We're known throughout the rest of the globe
For mystical beasts and creatures untold,
A tiny wee island the romans closed shut,
For fear of the Picts, all fucking nuts.

What many don't know is that whales surf our waves
While dolphins partake. That our northernmost points
Hold blinding white sands, mountains as far
As your vision allows, a land built perfect for a little escape.
the picturesque land whether trees or concrete.

Warriors, inventors, adventurers too. restless humans
That will never be bound, a unicorn bloody chained
By a lion...but lions die and the unicorns live on,
Freedom will come for the lands once again,
Once it's people remember the lessons of then.
A nation of man, born to thrive, given a fire in
And the will to survive, the fire burns true through all Scots blood
Even in the ones whose clan moved abroad. Lovliest people
so warm and welcome but Ask if we're English,
find out at your Peril.

Fire and beauty is only a part, we're musical,
Loving, creative and loud, we love to
Dance and throw each other around.

Keen on a pint and a laugh and a chat,
Keen on friendships and lovers and art,
We're more than just jimmy with his ginger wee hat,
We're beautiful people with so much to give

So do come and see our country of gold, with
The kelpies and fairies and mysteries told,
You stand in our towns and you feel ancient roots,
You'll leave again with the wish to be a Celt.

Scotland the Brave
Tha agal Agam ort.

SCOTLAND
by @poetstale

If we ever get lost and our homes are no more
Meet me in Edinburgh / Not on New Year's Day,
but the one before

I'll be waiting for you on the Royal Mile
In my dark green tartan with eyes that beguile
If it's too cold out on the cobblestone street
Search all the pubs
You'll find me cozy, with my whiskey neat

You can ask the bagpiper, which way did she go?
And trust me, we danced together, so he'll know
My heart hurts I miss you / We can't go back home though

We'll begin life anew, be artists, create
Let me taste your whiskey tongue
And we'll sing Haud Hogmanay!
p.s.

SCOTLAND
by @lismcdermott

Scotland, a land of beauty and natures wealth,
Peatlands, wild moors of purple heather,
Crofters following tradition, working the land;
The peaks of the Highlands,
The dour atmosphere of Glencoe
Where Clan MacDonald met their doom;
In memory, pipes and drums play a lament,
A pibroch of a sad, wailing tune;
The blue seas and white sands of Mallaig,
Passage to Skye and isles beyond;
Blues, pinks, yellows and greens a vision to see,
Painted hues of the houses in the harbour at Portree.
Dancing to music last heard at Mairi's Wedding,
Fiddle and drum accompanying the ceildh,
Shouts and calls, kilts swinging as they dance;
This the land of my forefathers,
The Clan Campbell.

© Lis McDermott 2020

SCOTLAND
by @kuranya_a_poet_dreaming

He holds my heart, in kilted muse, sewing
tapestries of Kings and Queens into weary bones
and falling stars into lonely eyes. He resurrects
long forsaken castles where only ruins lay and fair
maidens gather around his Gaelic serenade with
bonnie heart, so proud and true; in echo over cliff
and sea. His soul filled with love so gently found,
nestled 'tween the breasts of Glasgow dawns and
closed eyed bagpipe lullabies, calling for me to
dreams once more. Scotland, mo leannan, my heart
is yours.

©kuranya ~ a poet dreaming

SCOTLAND
by @katekennypoetry

The place my heart never
Knew it needed to be
Where I found my true love
Who helped rediscover me
As I appreciated the thistle
That grows taller than the weeds
I learned the truth of durability
When I saw friends gather
For a blether and a cuppa
I felt the full warm embrace
And comfort accomplished
By one small cup of tea.
I loved the landscape and
I felt it loved me
For when I took a deep breath
Full of Scottish air
Although I was foreign
I could exhale security;
I found my new home.

SCOTLAND
by @poetrybyparkes

As I look upon the land of thistles and Irn Bru
I remember that my lineage traces itself here
A world away from London and it's airborne hue
Her landscape amazes every sightseer
I remember being in Fort William
One weirdly hypnotic night
Drinking whiskey and beer
With no angry face in sight
Dancing in an empty disco
Challenging the DJ to a duel
Whilst making sure I didn't mention football
Because that would be way too cruel
It's true that my head was decidedly sore
The next morning when I awoke
Those eggs on my plate danced and jiggled
As if they were part of some elaborate joke
Eventually Ben Nevis called
A memory never to be forgotten
There were tears on the way up
And even more when we reached the bottom
We drove home the next day
Our heads slightly fuzzier than we'd have planned
Hangovers in excess
From only the beers please understand
It's true though
She leaves her mark on you
A part of Scotland lives on in me
Even if it's the wrong shade of blue

@poetrybyparkes

SCOTLAND
by @autumnalfyre

Chan eil ach beagan Gàidhlig agam.
I stumble through Gaelic from phrasebooks
and what that funny green owl has taught me
But I don't watch Outlander for the language
as much as I do to imagine Jamie Fraser
calling me a bonny lass
and telling me *Dinna fash*
I wonder what he has under that kilt
Scotland is a fantasy for me
Foggy moors and clans in tartans
Bagpipes and thistle flowers
Land of myths, like selkies,
unicorns and the Loch Ness monster
Most of my favorite bands are Scottish
Must be something in the water there
to have such music in one area
Scotch whiskey is the water of life
so pour me a glass of *uisge-beatha*
We'll say *Slàinte* and drink
like every day is Hogmanay
Tha gaol agam ort, Alba

@autumnalfyre

TONGUE
by @museofdarkness

Your smile is liquid starlight,
Whirling in dimples deep,
Turning into syrup sweet,
Poured into my mouth parched,
Through that flavourful tongue
of yours.

TONGUE
by @caitlinjadepoetry

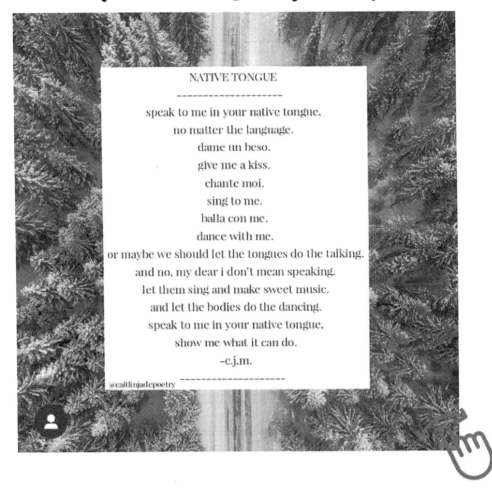

NATIVE TONGUE
----

speak to me in your native tongue,
no matter the language.
dame un beso.
give me a kiss.
chante moi.
sing to me.
baila con me.
dance with me.
or maybe we should let the tongues do the talking.
and no, my dear i don't mean speaking.
let them sing and make sweet music.
and let the bodies do the dancing.
speak to me in your native tongue,
show me what it can do.
-c.j.m.

@caitlinjadepoetry

TONGUE
by @secretwriter1427

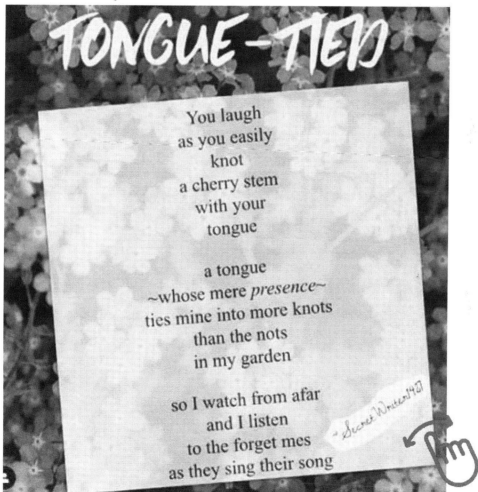

TONGUE-TIED

You laugh
as you easily
knot
a cherry stem
with your
tongue

a tongue
~whose mere *presence*~
ties mine into more knots
than the nots
in my garden

so I watch from afar
and I listen
to the forget mes
as they sing their song

TONGUE
by @sandra_change

TONGUE TWISTER MISTER

You are my tongue twister
My little big boss mister
Your dark eyes sparkle
You're as sharp as a shark

You call the day out for fight
Earth under your feet
You look so cheeky and proud
They all dance to your beat

You're clapping and tapping
When hit you're snapping
You're the one in charge
With a battery never low
You're a twister on a march
As dawn breaks you hit the show

You're hardcore energetic
Never apologetic
You're my favourite tongue
twister
My little big boss - A Mister!

SANDRA HOLT-ĆUŽE

TONGUE
by @dr.inkwright

"Tongue"

I felt cast out
It's unfortunate isn't it?
My heart spoke to her with a gentle request
Yet, instead of receiving kind reply I was emotionally met
with doubtful tone
Alone in a mental space where my face couldn't bear
what was spoken

A token of her love would have sufficed, but a [ton] of
emotions poured out from this broken fountain
I [gue]ss what is left isn't much to her
What crept into my mind were angered thoughts
Taught to me by those like her, who involuntarily showed
me the way
The path to become a heartbreaker
They make it look like a piece of cake
But the knife they used to cut isn't made of metal

IG: @dr.inkwright

TONGUE
by @littleblackheartpoetry

Lick me with your delicate words
Savor my taste upon your tongue
Serenade me with your sweetest songs
For I am about to become undone
Seek me out by taste alone
From sweetened nectar to salty sweat
Then by touch feel my honey skin
As you rev me up like a red Corvette

 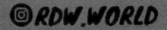

TONGUE
by @kipyard.rudling

[TON(IC WATER, GIN
CONCOCTION TO SLUR AND SIN
MADE HER WORDS GO RO)GUE]

- KR

ABOUT THE AUTHOR

"Like some kind of semi-aquatic mammal, I've always felt I don't quite fit in, and I struggle to swim in certain streams for too long. I'm certainly not the most adaptable or flexible soul, and sometimes you'll spot me, clinging stubbornly to my clumsy armbands and hoping for the best. Try as I might, I'm always halfway in-between. But I do have a certain luminosity about me; my character dances from time to time, and ever occasionally, my personality shines through and sticks in people's minds. I have an aura of sorts and as a writer, artist and human, I hope that counts for something."

RDW

Ryan Daniel Warner, is a self-styled 'Writer, Artist and Human' hailing from Northern England - the 'Lake District' to be precise. He owns the Instagram account, @rdw.world, and the website www.rdw.world, which both showcase his various projects related heavily to poetry, writing and wordplay.

His debut work, 'White Book' – the first in a series of 'Colours' will be available soon, in paperback and e-book format, while this 'Poetry 365' anthology will be released each month, featuring the work of a very talented collection of poets that became involved with his poetry prompts on Instagram.

Ryan would also like you to know that he hates speaking in third person about himself, or pretending that somebody else has written the above, so he will end this anthology, characteristically, in first person by simply saying

Thank you to all involved.
To those who wrote such wonderful pieces,
and to those who had the pleasure of reading them.

PLEASE SHOW YOUR SUPPORT FOR THE AMAZING POETS INVOLVED IN THIS EDITION OF 'POETRY 365' BY FOLLOWING THEM ON INSTAGRAM AND CHECKING OUT THEIR WORK.

Printed in Great Britain
by Amazon